Diversity Plans and Programs

SPEC KITS

Supporting Effective Library Management for Over Thirty-five Years

Committed to assisting research and academic libraries in the continuous improvement of management systems, ARL has worked since 1970 to gather and disseminate the best practices for library needs. As part of its commitment, ARL maintains an active publications program best known for its SPEC Kits. Through the Collaborative Research/Writing Program, librarians work with ARL staff to design SPEC surveys and write publications. Originally established as an information source for ARL member libraries, the SPEC Kit series has grown to serve the needs of the library community worldwide.

What are SPEC Kits?

Published six times per year, SPEC Kits contain the most valuable, up-to-date information on the latest issues of concern to libraries and librarians today. They are the result of a systematic survey of ARL member libraries on a particular topic related to current practice in the field. Each SPEC Kit contains an executive summary of the survey results; survey questions with tallies and selected comments; the best representative documents from survey participants, such as policies, procedures, handbooks, guidelines, Web sites, records, brochures, and statements; and a selected reading list—both print and online sources—containing the most current literature available on the topic for further study.

Subscribe to SPEC Kits

Subscribers tell us that the information contained in SPEC Kits is valuable to a variety of users, both inside and outside the library. SPEC Kit purchasers use the documentation found in SPEC Kits as a point of departure for research and problem solving because they lend immediate authority to proposals and set standards for designing programs or writing procedure statements. SPEC Kits also function as an important reference tool for library administrators, staff, students, and professionals in allied disciplines who may not have access to this kind of information.

SPEC Kits can be ordered directly from the ARL Publications Distribution Center. To order, call **(301) 362-8196**, fax **(301) 206-9789**, e-mail **pubs@arl.org**, or go to **http://www.arl.org/resources/pubs/**.

Information on SPEC Kits and the SPEC survey program can be found at **http://www.arl.org/resources/pubs/spec/index.shtml**. The executive summary for each kit after December 1993 can be accessed free of charge at **http://www.arl.org/resources/pubs/spec/complete.shtml**.

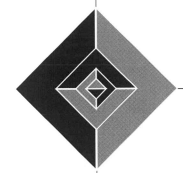

SPEC Kit 319

Diversity Plans and Programs
October 2010

Charlene Maxey-Harris

Diversity Librarian

University of Nebraska-Lincoln

Toni Anaya

Multicultural Studies Librarian

University of Nebraska-Lincoln

ASSOCIATION OF RESEARCH LIBRARIES

Series Editor: Lee Anne George

SPEC Kits are published by the

Association of Research Libraries
21 Dupont Circle, NW, Suite 800
Washington, DC 20036-1118
P (202) 296-2296 F (202) 872-0884
http://www.arl.org/resources/pubs/spec/
pubs@arl.org

ISSN 0160 3582

ISBN 1-59407-853-X
978-1-59407-853-8

SPEC Kit 319

Diversity Plans and Programs
October 2010

SURVEY RESULTS

REPRESENTATIVE DOCUMENTS

Diversity Group Charge

Diversity Programs

Recruitment Programs

Job Descriptions

SELECTED RESOURCES

SURVEY RESULTS

EXECUTIVE SUMMARY

Introduction

In 1990, ARL published SPEC Kit 165 *Cultural Diversity Programming in ARL Libraries* and SPEC Kit 167 *Minority Recruitment and Retention in ARL Libraries*. Both of these documents provided a wealth of information about library programs and services that addressed the needs of a diverse user group, minority staff recruitment and retention strategies, and approaches to managing an ethnically/culturally diverse workforce. While survey results in those SPEC Kits indicated that progress had been made since the 1960s, respondents indicated they thought there was much more to do to ensure that academic and research library staff are representative of all cultural, ethnic, religious, and racial groups, as well as those who have been discriminated against for their gender, sexual orientation, age, or disability.

Over the past ten years, several libraries have obtained funding to support recruitment strategies aimed at increasing the number of librarians from ethnically/culturally underrepresented groups in academic and research libraries, as well as promoting advancement within the organization. Libraries have also begun to put into practice policies and procedures to create more inclusive workplaces incorporating diverse staff, programs, and services. National recruitment initiatives, such as the ARL Initiative to Recruit a Diverse Workforce and the Leadership & Career Development Program, have been created to address the need to recruit minority librarians to the profession and advance them into leadership positions in ARL member libraries. During that time, the number of diversity or multicultural groups at the local, state, and national levels also appears to have increased.

The main purpose of this survey was to explore what other progress has been made in ARL member libraries to recruit and retain a diverse workforce and to identify the existence and content of diversity plan documents; the strategies they use to increase the number of ethnically/culturally diverse librarians in the profession and in their libraries; the elements of programs that successfully support an inclusive workplace; the people, groups, and/or committees responsible for overseeing the programs; and how libraries are assessing the effectiveness and success of such programs. The survey was conducted between March 15 and April 28, 2010. Forty-nine of the 124 ARL member institutions completed the survey for a response rate of 40%. All but one of the respondents is from an academic library.

Diversity Plans

A diversity plan may include a statement of diversity values or goals for the library, a description of strategies for recruiting ethnically/culturally diverse staff to the library and retaining them once they are hired, an outline of programs that promote ethnic/cultural sensitivity in the workplace, results from a work climate assessment, and other similar elements. It may be a stand-alone document or part of a broader document, such as a library strategic plan or an institution-wide diversity document. Thirty-six of the responding libraries (73%) stated they have a diversity plan as described above. Some of these documents pull together all of the activities related to diversity into one strategic plan.

Of these 36 respondents, 13 reported that their parent institutions were responsible for initiating the development of the plan. In 11 cases, the parent institution and the library were jointly responsible. At the other 12 institutions, the library administration and/ or human resources unit initiated plan development. In addition, two libraries identified the initiators as the parent institution affirmative action office/department and a system-wide request originating with central university administration. Other comments suggest the initiative came from a staff committee within the library.

Slightly more than a third of the diversity plans (13 or 37%) are stand-alone documents. Almost an equal number (12 or 34%) are part of a broader parent institution document such as a strategic plan, annual report, or an affirmative action or equal employment opportunity (EEO) report. Four are part of a library strategic plan. Based on the comments, a few library plans are stand-alone but are based on an institution-wide document.

The components of diversity plans vary among the responding organizations, but the majority of the plans contain

- Goals and strategies
- Mission or values statements
- Definition of diversity
- Organizational responsibility/accountability

Some diversity plans include a diversity-related committee charge (34%), a description of diversity programs (29%), and other elements such as assessment strategies, and policies and procedures (i.e., EEO, affirmative action) related to search committees.

Clearly, research institutions have been working to create a more culturally diverse organization, but apparently few have had a plan that guided their activities. Prior to 1990, only two of the 30 responding libraries had a diversity plan. Within the ten-year span 1990 to 1999, only four others developed a document. The rate of development has begun to change, though. Between 2000 and 2004, six more libraries developed a plan. Since 2005, seventeen libraries (57%) have

developed a diversity plan; six of those within the last year. The creation of such a plan indicates a strong commitment to diversity within the organization.

A major factor in the success of a diversity plan is its implementation. Survey results show that responsibility for implementation is often shared by human resources officers and a diversity committee or a related group (16 responses or 44%). In several cases, they are joined by a diversity officer, staff development officer, or multicultural librarian. At ten libraries, the human resources officer has primary responsibility, but works with other administrators and various library committees. At four others, the diversity committee takes charge of implementation. In a few cases, implementation is at the campus level, such as the vice provost for equal opportunity, president's office, campus human resources, and search committees.

Implementing a diversity plan sets the course for progress, but may be inadequate without a process to review its effectiveness and update its contents as goals and strategies change. Eighty-one percent of the survey respondents periodically review their plans, typically on an annual cycle. A few report a review cycle between two and five years. Some libraries indicated that their reviews were on hold and are currently waiting for more information from the parent institution.

Creating a diversity plan implies an intention to distribute it to stakeholders. Survey results indicate diversity plans are disseminated to library staff and the university community in a multitude of ways. At least half of the responding libraries share their plan through the library Web site and/or include it in a university document. Twenty-five percent discuss the library's vision for diversity during new employee orientation. Three libraries (8%) incorporate this information into the library staff handbook. Other methods include posting the diversity plan or vision on an internal staff webpage or wiki. Diversity forums and discussions are also used to disseminate information. In contrast, one library only submits their diversity document to the library administration. Some libraries submit their information as a report to the parent institution's EEO or affirmation action policy office and rely on that office to inform employees through presentations, internal brochures and memorandums, and posters.

Diversity Librarian

Twenty years after the creation of positions focused on fostering diversity in libraries, one would expect the number of these types of positions to have increased. In 1990, SPEC Kit 165 included six position descriptions that contained diversity-related duties and expectations. Responses to the current survey show only a slight increase: three multicultural librarians and seven diversity officers were reported. These results are supported by Lori Mestre's recent research into positions that primarily focus on diversity and multicultural issues in academic libraries. She found there were "only 14 out of 107 ARL libraries in the US" that had a full-time dedicated diversity librarian, even when she expanded her search for job titles to include "diversity librarians, multicultural librarians, outreach librarian for multicultural services, Ethnic Studies librarian, and similar titles." (Mestre, 2010, p. xiv)

Diversity Committees

While there are few "diversity librarians," the survey results indicate that more than half of the responding libraries have a diversity-related committee. These committees provide library staff an opportunity to work towards creating a more inclusive workplace. Human resources officers often lead or are at least an ex-officio member of the committee. At the majority of libraries, the committee and HR officer share the responsibility for developing and implementing the diversity plan, and planning and delivering ongoing programs to promote an inclusive work environment. It became apparent when reviewing the documents submitted by survey respondents that in the 21st century the role of diversity committees has moved beyond these original roles to advising library and university administration on diversity issues, creating recruitment plans, and assisting with training of search committees.

Programs to Promote an Inclusive Workplace

Approximately half of the responding libraries have ongoing presentations and/or workshops on issues relevant to promoting an inclusive workplace. Another seven (14%) have had at least one-time presentations and eight plan to develop programs. Ten others (20%) have not developed any workshops or programming, yet. The number of programs ranges from 1 to 20 a year with an average of four per year. In some cases, library programs are open to the campus community.

Topics addressed during these programs and/or workshops include race and ethnicity (78%), physical disabilities (66%), sexual orientation (53%), language barriers (50%), and gender and/or age discrimination (47%). Other topics that have been addressed either within the library or through the university system are cross- or inter-cultural communication, cultural competencies, religion, affirmative action or equal opportunity, and social economics issues. Examples of large events that libraries have initiated include a sign language forum and an international party.

In addition to HR officers and diversity committees, staff development officers, diversity officers, and multicultural librarians are also involved with planning and delivering programs for library staff. Libraries also utilize the resources of the parent institution, taking advantage of programs that are open to all staff at the institution. Individuals and departments involved in planning and delivering diversity programming at the campus level include administrators, LGBTA centers, offices of disability services, and social justice programs.

Diversity Web Sites

Library Web sites are the face of the organization. This is the entryway for individuals to see what is important to the organization. It was refreshing to see the number of Web sites submitted for the survey that have information about diversity values and initiatives. A review of several sites revealed a wealth of information about diversity-related committees, goals and objectives, diversity plans, and resources that support multicultural research.

Recruitment Strategies

In 1990, SPEC Kit 167 asked recruitment questions about hiring activities, advertising available positions, and barriers to recruitment. At that time, active recruitment and rewriting job descriptions "so that minority applicants will not be discouraged" were identified as specific strategies to increase the diversity of job applicant pools.

Today, there are a wider variety of strategies. Of the libraries responding to this survey, 82% have employed strategies to specifically increase the pool of ethnically/culturally diverse job applicants. The top three most frequently reported strategies are targeting job ads to participants in ALA and ARL diversity recruitment programs (68%), supporting ARL diversity initiatives (60%), and training search committees to develop a diverse candidate pool (60%). Although 40 of the responding libraries have used a range of strategies to specifically increase the diversity of job applicant pools, only 21 found any of them particularly successful. Offering post-MLIS residency opportunities and recruiting from the five ALA ethnic caucuses are among the effective strategies. Other specific ways libraries are recruiting minority librarians include building alliances with the University of Arizona's Knowledge River Program, Hispanic Association of Colleges and Universities (HACU), Historically Black Colleges and Universities (HBCU), and LIS Access Midwest Program (LAMP), and attending local career fairs.

Eleven libraries identified particularly successful job advertising venues to increase the diversity of the applicant pool. Among the most effective and widely used method is advertising in publications and on electronic discussion lists targeted to ethnically and culturally diverse individuals, including the ALA ethnic caucus lists.

Along with successful strategies for the recruitment process, 44% of respondents identified recruitment barriers. The library's geographic location was the most common barrier to attracting a diverse pool of candidates, as were lack of qualified applicants and a general perception of a lack of diversity in the profession. Other barriers include obtaining racial and ethnic information from applicants and the lack of diverse students in MLIS programs interested in academic library positions.

Mentoring Programs

Though many ARL member libraries have mentoring programs, only four reported having a program that is specifically intended to help ethnically/culturally diverse librarians to attain advancement or tenure. Another five (10%) are planning to develop such a program. Mentoring within the ARL diversity initiatives and other leadership programs also provides support for these librarians outside their current positions.

Evaluation & Assessment

Only 11 respondents (22%) have developed any measures to evaluate the success of their efforts to recruit an ethnically/culturally diverse workforce, though nine (18%) plan to develop such measures in the future. Only three respondents have any measures to evaluate the success of retention efforts, but 11 intend to develop such measures.

To assess their recruitment efforts, some of the libraries are using the information in the affirmative action or EEO plan reports. At least one library is involved in a multi-year longitudinal study to investigate the efficacy of the current recruitment sponsored by ARL. Another library is targeting their recruitment efforts to MLIS programs with larger graduation rates by underrepresented students. An increase in the number of applicants from targeted schools will be the measure of success.

Workplace Climate

Just under half of the responding institutions have completed an assessment of the library climate; an additional eight (17%) are planning a climate assessment in the future. Most often, the assessment instrument was a survey developed by the library. Other surveys were developed by the parent institution or by outside vendors such as Gallup, ClimateQUAL™, and Towers Watson International Survey Research.

When asked if the assessment information was used to change the diversity plan or programs, 14 respondents (32%) reported they have used this information to provide guidance in their planning, though the majority (22 or 50%) has not used the information in this fashion. Two report that the university implements the survey and it is not library specific.

Conclusion

Successful diversity management requires a variety of tactics and strategies. Patricia Kreitz's research on diversity "best practices" centered on discovering organizations that have been working to define and assess progress. She found that the more levels of commitment within the organization, the stronger the commitment is to change the organization and to recognize the benefits. According to her findings, successful diversity initiatives require both top management leadership and employee commitment. The responses to this survey show there is strong support for diversity by both library and university administration at ARL member institutions. This inspires confidence that there will be a change in the workplace dynamics.

Lori Mestre argues there is a gap of services and responsibility without a full-time individual to oversee diversity outreach, collection development, reference and instruction, programming, and liaison responsibilities. However, many other levels of support and commitment are necessary to carry out the diversity plan and a committed leadership team at the institution level and within the library guarantees a strong, effective plan for diversity.

This survey indicates there has been a significant increase in the number of groups and committees formed to address diversity or inclusive workplace goals in the past ten years. Human resource officers share the responsibility of leading these committees and implementing diversity plans with diversity officers, staff development officers, multicultural librarians, and other library staff. Even without the presence of a primary, full-time individual responsible for diversity and multicultural activities, these endeavors are achieved when the library administration makes diversity everyone's responsibility.

In 2006, Courtney Young explored the presence of diversity Web information in the Committee on Institutional Cooperation (CIC), a small subset of large academic research libraries. Her research also looked at whether diversity information was located on top- or lower-level pages. Because only two of 13 libraries had top-level links to the diversity-related pages and very few had information about the diversity collections, she made several recommendations for libraries, including: place a link for diversity or multicultural topics in the top level page, provide contact information for the diversity individual or group, publicize diversity programs, and highlight information for persons with disabilities. While there is evidence that libraries are moving in this direction, more libraries should follow this advice since the willingness to publicly share their diversity plan and strategies via the Web site suggests a welcoming, inclusive environment in which to work, study, and be successful.

Recruiting and retaining a diverse workforce continues to be a challenge for libraries. It is evident that research libraries are committed to actively recruit librarians from underrepresented ethnic/racial groups and have employed specific strategies to increase the diversity of applicant pools. What is not known is how many of the open searches have resulted in new hires of minority librarians. At this point, it is difficult to acknowledge strides that might have been made because of the lack of recruitment assessment tools.

Very few libraries are designing mentoring programs specifically for librarians from underrepresented ethnic or cultural groups. Many of the libraries responding to this survey have informal or formal mentoring programs for all librarians but rely on external professional development programs, such as those sponsored by the ALA ethnic caucuses, to provide mentoring opportunities for librarians from underrepresented groups. They also turn to skill building opportunities offered by the University of Minnesota Training Institute for Early Career Librarians and ARL's Leadership & Career Development Program for training to advance these librarians to leadership positions.

As libraries continue to move forward in diversity activities, more statistics need to be mined from reports such as the *ARL Annual Salary Survey* and ALA *Diversity Counts* to actually validate the efforts of the recruiting and hiring of staff and librarians from underrepresented racial, ethnic, and cultural groups. The development of more assessment tools will be crucial to provide supporting evidence of change. Academic libraries are also looking forward to the development of guidelines for cultural competencies by the Association of College and Research Libraries Racial and Ethnic Diversity Committee. These guidelines will extend the inclusion of skills and behaviors necessary to support a working environment that acknowledges the strength in having multicultural and diverse individuals in the organization.

SURVEY QUESTIONS AND RESPONSES

The SPEC survey on Diversity Plans and Programs was designed by **Toni Anaya**, Multicultural Studies Librarian, and **Charlene Maxey-Harris**, Diversity Librarian, University of Nebraska-Lincoln. These results are based on data submitted by 49 of the 124 ARL member libraries (40%) by the deadline of April 28, 2010. The survey's introductory text and questions are reproduced below, followed by the response data and selected comments from the respondents.

In 1990, ARL published SPEC Kit 165 *Cultural Diversity Programming in ARL Libraries* and SPEC Kit 167 *Minority Recruitment and Retention in ARL Libraries*. Both of these documents provided a wealth of information about library programs and services that addressed the needs of a diverse user group, minority staff recruitment and retention strategies, and approaches to managing an ethnically/culturally diverse workforce. While the survey results indicated that progress had been made since the 1960s, respondents indicated they thought there was much more to do to ensure that academic and research library staff are representative of all cultural, ethnic, religious, and racial groups, as well as those who have been discriminated against for their gender, sexual orientation, age, or disability.

Since 1990, several libraries have obtained funding to support strategies, such as post-LIS diversity residencies, to increase the number of minority librarians in academic and research librarians and promote their advancement within the organization. ARL also started programs, such as the Initiative to Recruit a Diverse Workforce and the Leadership & Career Development Program, to address the need to recruit minority librarians to the profession and advance them into leadership positions in ARL libraries. During that time the number of diversity or multicultural groups at the local, state, and national levels also appears to have increased.

The main purpose of this survey is to explore what other progress has been made in ARL member libraries to recruit and retain a diverse workforce and to identify:

- the existence and content of diversity plan documents in ARL member libraries;
- the strategies they use to increase the number of ethnically/culturally diverse librarians in the profession and in their libraries;
- the elements of programs that successfully support an inclusive workplace;
- the people, groups, and/or committees responsible for overseeing the programs;
- and how libraries are assessing the effectiveness and success of such programs.

The survey will also gather documentation about ARL member libraries' diversity plans and programs, and provide another benchmark for progress towards diversity goals.

DIVERSITY PLAN

A diversity plan may include a statement of diversity values or goals for the library, a description of strategies for recruiting ethnically/culturally diverse staff to the library and retaining them once they are hired, an outline of programs that promote ethnic/cultural sensitivity in the workplace, results from a work climate assessment, and other similar elements. It may be a stand-alone document or part of a broader document, such as a library strategic plan or an institution-wide diversity document.

1. Does your library have a diversity plan as described above to guide recruitment and retention efforts? N=49

Yes	36	73%
No	13	27%

If you answered Yes, please answer the following questions.

If you answered No, please skip to the Recruitment Strategies section of the survey.

2. If yes, who instigated the development of the plan? Check all that apply. N=36

Parent institution	24	67%
Library administration	22	61%
Library Human Resources officer/unit	7	19%
Other	7	19%

Please specify other instigator.

Faculty and Staff Affirmative Action Office.

Feedback from staff members led to creation of Library Diversity Council in 2006.

Joint Committee on Affirmative Action.

Millennium Report Oversight Committee.

The university maintains Affirmative Action Compliance Plans.

The university system and the campus have diversity statements.

Working with the Diversity Committee, the HR Librarian developed guidelines for efforts at recruitment and retention for professional staff.

3. In which year was the diversity plan developed? N=30

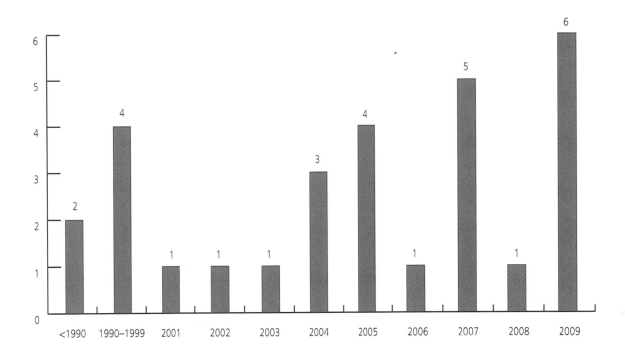

4. Is the plan a stand-alone document or part of a broader document? N=35

Stand-alone document	13	37%
Part of a broader parent institution document	12	34%
Part of a broader library document	4	11%
Other	6	17%

Please describe the other document.

Employment Equity Policy No. 2; Advertising of Position Vacancies Policy No. 20 ; Statement on Respectful Environment for Students, Faculty, and Staff.

Encompassed by the parent institution's policy: Overview of Equity Procedures.

It is a stand-alone document that is based on a university-wide document, titled University Wide Diversity Plan.

It is stand alone, but it articulates a institutional strategic plan: University Strategic Diversity Plan.

The following is included in position descriptions for the university faculty: Texas Tech is an Affirmative Action /Equal Opportunity Employer. We strongly encourage applications from women, minorities, and veterans, and we consider the needs of dual career couples.

We are governed by the university diversity plan: Department of Institutional Diversity Program/Goals.

If the plan is part of a broader document, please identify the title of that document.

Part of a broader parent institution document

Annual EEO/Diversity Profile: Utilization Analysis.

Diversity Action Plan for the University.

Diversity Annual Report.

Diversity statement.

University Affirmative Action Report.

University Equal Opportunity Plan; University Diversity Strategic Plan.

Path to Prominence: Strategic Plan for the University.

Strategic Plan; University Plan--Principles of Community.

The university maintains Affirmative Action Compliance Plans.

The University Diversity Statement; University Strategic Plan for Diversity; University's Principles of Community.

There is currently a Principal's Task Force on Diversity Excellence and Community Engagement.

University EEO Policy and Procedures; Library System - Vision, Mission Statement; Council of Librarians - Code specifically in relation to Search and Screening Committees.

Part of a broader library document

Libraries Strategic Plan

Libraries' Strategic Plan

Library Strategic Plan, 2006

University Library In Pursuit of Our Strategic Vision 2005–2010

Stand-alone document

Not part of the university plan, but follows from the university initiative and 2006 report of the System-Wide Academic Task Force: Diversity.

5. Is this plan reviewed and/or updated periodically? N=36

Yes	29	81%
No	2	6%
Not yet, but it will be	5	14%

If the plan is or will be reviewed periodically, please describe the frequency of review and revision. N=29

Reviewed periodically

Annually (12 responses)

5-year cycle (2 responses)

As determined by Board of Governors.

Created in 2006, updated in 2008–09, plan to revisit every 2 years going forward.

Each plan is for a five-year period. A mid-term progress report and a final progress report are prepared for every plan period.

It has been reviewed once in three years, but the plan is to review it every year at the university level.

Review is within the parent institutions' processes.

So far it has been updated in March 2009 and August 2009.

The Affirmative Action Compliance plans are reviewed and updated annually.

The Diversity Action Plan is a living document. It has been widely reviewed, revised and will continue to undergo improvement. The Libraries' Millennium Report Oversight Committee reviews plan annually.

The Diversity Committee reviews and revises our plan annually.

The plan is reviewed and revised on a yearly basis.

The report is distributed annually from Human Resources and reviewed with the Dean of each school to discuss progress and efforts related to diversity.

Uncertain, done by university administration.

Not yet, but it will be

Ideally the plan will be updated every 3–4 years.

The current diversity goals were created for a 5-year time period (2007–2012).

We will conduct a local review every other year, with our first year beginning July 2010.

Comments

Library Strategic Plan and Library Mission, Vision, Values both refer to Respect.

See: The Path to Prominence through Diversity: University of Delaware Diversity Task Force Final Report. (February 2009) http://www.udel.edu/aboutus/diversity-finalreport.pdf

The goals need to be revised this coming year. There is an aim to integrate these goals with the library's next 5-year strategic plan.

The library looks at/reviews it annually and as needed to guide our work in diversity.

The university, under the leadership of the president, announced in February 2010 that he was forming a Council on Diversity and Inclusion with a new Associate Provost to be appointed Spring 2010.

There are many resources available on the University Diversity Web pages.

We did not update the plan in 2008/2009 because the university will be requiring diversity plans and we want to make sure ours follows those requirements. We are also involved in the Library Scorecard Pilot and want to see how that fits.

6. **Please identify the elements that are included in the plan, such as statement of values, recruitment goals and/or strategy, description of diversity programs, etc. Check all that apply. N=35**

Goals & Strategies	30	86%
Mission or Values Statement	25	71%
Diversity definition	24	69%
Organization responsibility & accountability	20	57%
Committee charge	12	34%
Description of diversity programs for library staff	10	29%
Other element	7	20%

Please describe the other element(s) in the plan.

Assessment strategies and timeline.

Compliance plan for the university, i.e.; EEO policies.

Partnerships with other university departments and programs.

Reference to related policies.

Texas Tech is an Affirmative Action/Equal Opportunity Employer. We Strongly encourage applications from women, minorities, and veterans, and we consider the needs of dual career couples.

The document is focuses mainly on a utilization analysis and goals for diversity. The plan has components but is not a fully structured plan.

The intent is stated within the Diversity Program. The Code for the Council of Librarians describes the responsibility of the chairperson of any librarian searches in regards to diversity and EEO compliance. The Mission and Vision Statement for the library system states our value of diversity.

7. **What group/individual is responsible for implementing the diversity plan? Check all that apply. N=36**

HR/Personnel officer	26	72%
Diversity Committee or other related group	20	56%
Diversity officer	7	19%
Staff Development officer	4	11%
Multicultural Librarian	3	8%
Other individual or group	22	61%

Please describe the other individual or group.

Academic Programs division of the library (largest division, core collections and services responsibilities), libraries leadership from all areas.

All library leadership, as well as managers/supervisors are responsible for demonstrating and leading diversity and inclusion in their organizations, reflected in performance management and recognition processes, as well as the library's promotion review process.

Campus HR, library HR, and library administration. All department heads are aware of diversity efforts.

Council of Librarians and all supervisors in selection process are tasked with ensuring that a diverse pool of candidates is considered.

Dean, Library Directors, Department Heads.

Director for Administrative Services; Diversity Task Force of 2010.

Director of Libraries and associate directors.

Employment Equity Director.

Every search committee for an academic position.

Individual directors.

Liaison to Diversity Team.

Libraries administration plays an active role, as well as the Diversity Committee.

Library Affirmative Action Representative.

President's office as well as search committees.

The Chancellor, together with her cabinet members, have delegated responsibility to all supervisory personnel, both faculty and administrative, to carry out the university's equal opportunity /affirmative action programs. However, overall responsibility rests with the Chancellor, through the Vice President of Human Services and the Associate Vice President, Chief Human Resources Officer.

There are elements to the plan to require the involvement of many Libraries' staff for successful implementation. Those are noted on the plan where appropriate.

University campus-level HR managers, deans/directors, department managers.

University Librarian.

University Diversity Advisory Board.

Various library committees, department heads along with other library administrative staff.

Vice Provost and May Morris Director of Libraries (this is the full title of the library dean position).

Vice Provost for Equal Opportunity, Vice Provost for Diversity and Inclusion, Academic Personnel Librarian, Assistant Director for Organizational Design and Learning.

Comments

Also support and partnership from University Office for Equity and Diversity.

Librarians Association of the University of California - Riverside division has a Committee on Diversity that also participates in carrying out the objectives of the Plan.

The AA representative is responsible for ensuring that appointments committees have an AA representative and that the AA plan is followed throughout the hiring process. Ultimately, however, the Office of the University Librarian is responsible for decanal oversight of the appointment process.

The HR Librarian serves as ex officio as chair for the Diversity Committee.

The HR officer chairs the Diversity Committee.

8. How does the library disseminate the diversity plan? Check all that apply. N=36

Posted on library Web site	19	53%
Included in a parent institution document	18	50%
Discussed/distributed during new employee orientation	9	25%
Included in information for job recruits	8	22%
Included in library staff handbook	3	8%
Other method(s)	15	42%

Please describe the other method(s) used to disseminate the plan.

Annual Memorandum from the Librarian of Congress to all LOC staff.

Disseminated through discussions with the Libraries executive committee and department heads.

Diversity forums are conducted with the dean's participation.

E-mail.

Included as part of the search process.

It is a document that was reviewed and approved by our faculty.

Posted on host institution's Web site.

Posted on library staff wiki.

Posted on library's internal Intranet.

Posted on the staff wiki, which serves as the staff handbook.

Posted on university Web site and distributed to libraries' leadership team.

Statement goes with job descriptions.

Submitted to EVC and Chancellor with UL evaluation on an annual basis.

The university has brought and will continue to bring its Equal Employment Opportunity (EEO) Policy to the attention of its employees, where applicable and appropriate. Further, all necessary steps will be taken to ensure that the university's personnel, management, and other appropriate individuals are fully apprised of the university's EEO Policy and the existence of this Affirmative Action Plan (AAP). The AAP will be discussed and reviewed in supervisory and management meetings. Periodic reviews with the university's supervisory, managerial, and other employees, as appropriate, will be conducted to determine the effectiveness of various aspects of this AAP. EEO posters will remain placed in conspicuous locations.

Through system-wide and campus Web sites.

Comments

Candidates who apply for librarian positions are made aware of the Employment Equity Policy and they are asked to self-identify.

Library does not distribute its own diversity plans except to upper level library administration. It builds on the campus plan.

The methods, relevant to the university, by which the EEO Policy is internally disseminated have been examined and those currently in effect are referenced below: • Information that covers the progress and activities of the Affirmative Action Program is regularly disseminated and is posted on the Office of Human Resources Web site. • The Office of Human Resources continually offer seminars and instructional programs designed to familiarize each individual in a supervisory role with various Federal guidelines and statutes governing Equal Opportunity and Affirmative Action. • The Associate Vice President, Chief Human Resources Officer, and the Director of Diversity and Resolution Processes make regular presentations related to the mission of Affirmative Action to various sectors of the university community. • Each administrator and supervisor is notified and held accountable for compliance with the Affirmative Action Program, and each must inform supervising personnel of the AAP goals and requirements, thus monitoring their own departmental compliance. • The university has informed and continues to inform all employees, management, and others that it does not tolerate or sanction harassment of any employee because of race, color, religion, age, sex, disability, veteran status, marital status, national origin, sexual orientation, or sexual identity. • Union representatives have been informed of the EEO Policy. • Nondiscrimination clauses have been included in all university collective bargaining agreements. These provisions are reviewed periodically to ensure compliance. • The university posts its EEO Policy in the Administrative Personnel Manual and on the university's Web site and will continue to do so in the future. • Internal university brochures, manuals, etc., will depict minorities, non-minorities, and females. • The university encourages employees to bring questions, comments, or complaints regarding its EEO Policy and AAP to the Office of Human Resources. Specifically, questions, comments, or complaints should be directed to the Director, Diversity and Resolution Processes.

RECRUITMENT STRATEGIES

9. Has your library employed any strategies specifically to increase the pool of ethnically/culturally diverse job applicants? N=49

Yes	40	82%
No	7	14%
Not yet, but we plan to	2	4%

If you answered Yes, please answer the following questions.

If you answered No or Not yet, please skip to the Programs to Promote an Inclusive Workplace section of the survey.

10. Please indicate which of the following strategies your library has used. Check all that apply. N=40

Targets job ads to participants in programs such as Spectrum, ARL Initiatives, etc.	27	68%
Supports ARL initiatives intended to attract ethnically/culturally diverse individuals to the profession	24	60%
Trains search committee members on how to develop an ethnically/culturally diverse candidate pool	24	60%
Partners with professional, local, or student organizations to aide in the recruitment of ethnically/culturally diverse individuals to the profession	14	35%
Offers a post-LIS residency program for ethnically/culturally diverse individuals	12	30%
Partners with LIS program to offer a practicum experience to ethnically/culturally diverse individuals	8	20%
Provides financial support to ethnically/culturally diverse staff to attend LIS programs	5	13%
Supports LIS scholarships intended to attract ethnically/culturally diverse individuals to the profession	4	10%
Offers a pre-LIS fellowship or internship program for ethnically/culturally diverse individuals	4	10%
Other strategy	14	35%

Please describe the other strategy.

Advertises in the five minority caucus newsletters and job lists.

Note that any state-funded programs cannot be restricted to only ethnically/culturally diverse individuals.

Previously had a pre-LIS internship program, but this has been redesigned and become the post-LIS residency program.

Search committee members contact colleagues at other institutions, call prospective candidates to encourage application, and register positions with the university system's applicant clearinghouse.

Send job announcements to minority caucuses of ALA job sites and library schools.

Specifically targeting minority venues for advertising vacancies.

Sponsors & conducts Leadership Institute for Early Career Librarians from Under-Represented Groups; hires high school students in city's summer Step Up program; participates in ALA social, committee and educational activities.

Targets job ads to specific communities.

Targets listservs and publications reviewed mainly by ethnically/culturally diverse individuals.

Tuition reimbursement is available to all staff members; targeted recruiting to student groups and minority listservs; participation with ARL diversity events at ALA and hosted luncheon; International Associates Program (residency); local community outreach to increase awareness of profession (Family & Community Archives Project with Co-op High School and Manuscripts & Archives staff; Medical Library with Career High School). In the past, we have participated in events such as NAACP career fair in NYC and hosted Librarians in Residence and fellows mentored by the University Librarian.

University's Target of Opportunity Plan: Libraries identify outstanding diverse professionals and university provides multi-year financial support for their hire.

Use of Web sites and listservs targeted to diverse populations are used to post open positions.

Utilizes alliance with the Hispanic Association of Colleges and Universities (HACU) for direct recruitment. Assessing/reviewing diversity in applicant pool in agency merit selection processes.

We are currently participating in a broad survey of ARL libraries re: recruitment efforts to attract diverse pools of qualified applicants.

11. **Have any of these strategies been particularly successful for increasing the pool of ethnically/culturally diverse job applicants? N=37**

Yes	21	57%
No	16	43%

If yes, please briefly describe the more successful strategies.

Advertising.

Assessing applicant pool diversity in selection process and HACU.

Broader and targeting advertising, advertising internally. Have seen increased diversity in applicant pool, and also notice that there is more diversity in the early career professional population, so difficult to attribute causal relationship to one approach or another.

Current recruitment for cataloger with Japanese language required and Korean language preferred yielded a large number of culturally diverse applicants.

Making sure the search committee members are aware of the goals and actively push this information out. Training is also helpful.

Our post-LIS residency program has a hiring rate double the ARL overall rate for ethnic/cultural diversity.

Participation in ARL Leadership and Career Development Program; Recruiting from LIS programs known for diversity (e.g., Knowledge River).

Post LIS Fellowship Program has been successful for over 25 years in the recruitment and retention of ethnically/diverse librarians. Program has been a model for academic libraries throughout the country. Search committees have been strong allies in making sure candidate pools are diverse and that committees follow affirmative action guidelines.

Post-LIS residency increases our diversity profile. I am in the process of acquiring data to determine if other strategies have resulted in increases in the diversity of applicant pools. Pre-LIS program resulted in hiring 3 tenure-track hires.

Successful recruitment of a minority librarian from the ALA Black Caucus publicity (she was also a Spectrum scholar).

Support of ARL initiatives, particularly partnership with ARL Initiative to Recruit a Diverse Workforce which provides participants with a behind-the-scenes look at an academic research library during a two-day onsite visit with costs fully covered by the library.

Target of Opportunity has helped us to hire one librarian and we have plans for several more.

Targeted advertising, especially listservs, and working with the library school on our campus to recruit diverse candidates to academic libraries.

The library currently has two Resident Librarians from underrepresented population.

The Pauline A. Young Residency is a 2-year, post-LIS minority recruitment program that offers a breadth of professional experience in a highly automated academic research library setting. The 2-year residency is designed to meet both the professional goals and interests of the resident as well as the service and operational priorities of the University of Delaware Library. In the first year, the resident works with librarians in several key areas of the library, gaining broadly based experience. In the second year, the resident selects an area of responsibility that builds on this foundation and furthers his or her specific professional goals. See http://www2.lib.udel.edu/personnel/residency/index.html for more information.

We believe that the use of the various listserves has provided an opportunity for a broader applicant pool as well as our own staff's outreach in recruiting efforts. Listservs used are listjobs@drexel.edu, listjobs, ILI-L@ala.org.

We were able to hire several of the post-LIS residency individuals.

12. Has your library encountered any perceived barriers to increasing the pool of ethnically/culturally diverse candidates?   N=39

Yes	17	44%
No	22	56%

If yes, please briefly describe the barrier and any success the library has had in overcoming it.

As a profession, we are not diverse across a number of measures. We are working with the library school on our campus to recruit diverse LIS students to the school and to academic libraries through a competitive two-year associates program for students working in the library.

Geographic location is a particular issue. Being located in central Pennsylvania away from major metropolitan centers sometimes makes it difficult to attract a diverse candidate pool.

Geographical barrier - our city is sometimes perceived as an environment in which ethnically/culturally diverse candidates may not want to live. We try to counter that perception by offering tours of the area, contacts with campus faculty and staff who are ethnically/culturally diverse, and allowing for return visits to the area.

Hiring freezes. Geography - not urban. Predominantly white institution. Lack of exit interview data.

Just a limit in the number of diverse candidates interested in academic librarianship.

Location/climate.

Louisville, KY may not have a reputation for diversity that would attract a diverse pool of applicants for open positions. Having the National Diversity in Libraries Conference here in 2008 helped to change that perception.

Many candidates who apply do not meet the minimum qualifications, especially around having an MLS or one that is accredited by ALA.

Most applicants opt not to report ethnicity data. To date, we've not overcome that issue.

Not hiring much right now; reduced benefits for managerial & professional staff starting in July 2010. Current economic environment limits funding for fee-based outreach, advertising, or travel, sponsoring paid interns or fellows, etc.

Our larger community is not very diverse at all. We are currently seeking input from minority professionals about ways to overcome this barrier.

Reluctance to consider living and working in a small city. Bringing participants in ARL Initiatives to Recruit a Diverse Workforce to visit library has resulted in applications from participants.

Salary ranges.

Staff resistance to thinking of importance of diversity within pools.

The cost of living in this region can be quite a barrier across the board. This remains difficult to overcome.

The pool of professional librarians for certain positions, Asian language specialists, is limited.

Unfortunately, the total percentage of diverse graduates from LIS programs has not increased.

13. Has your library discovered any particularly successful job advertising venues for increasing the pool of ethnically/culturally diverse job applicants? N=38

Yes	11	29%
No	27	71%

If yes, please identify the venue(s).

Advertise in all a large number of diverse publications, listservs, etc. such as BCALA, CALA, APALA, Reforma, etc.

ALA minority caucus job sites.

Community newspaper postings.

Diversity-L.(listserve of LLAMA Diversity Officers Discussion Group), ARL initiatives, Spectrum.

Minority Caucuses.

Our current Libraries faculty and staff who are ethically/culturally diverse have been instrumental in our efforts to increase our pools.

Spectrum e-mail list is very useful for recruiting the residency position.

Student organizations, minority listservs of existing professional organizations (like SAA), IFLA, Canadian library schools, more urban library schools and alumni lists (Wayne State) although we try to reach most library schools with e-mail jobs lists.

Targeted listservs.

Targeted Publications and Web sites.

The University Office of Diversity posts all open positions on different cultural/ethnic Web sites. The library posts at different churches, local organizations and clubs that have an ethnic and culturally diverse membership.

PROGRAMS TO PROMOTE AN INCLUSIVE WORKPLACE

14. Has your library developed any presentations, workshops, programs, etc. for staff to promote an inclusive workplace? N=49

Yes, we have an ongoing program of presentations, workshops, etc.	24	49%
Yes, we have had one-time presentations, workshops, etc.	7	14%
No	10	20%
Not yet, but we plan to	8	16%

If you answered Yes, please answer the following questions.

If you answered No or Not yet, please continue to the Mentoring section of the survey.

15. Please indicate which of the following topics have been addressed in the presentations, workshops, programs, etc. Check all that apply. N=32

Race and ethnicity	25	78%
Physical disabilities	21	66%
Sexual orientation	17	53%
Language barriers	16	50%
Gender and/or age discrimination	15	47%
Other topic(s)	12	38%

Please describe the other topic(s).

Cross-cultural communication workshop for library staff.

Cultural competencies in the workplace. Campus Climate Initiatives. Micro-aggressions.

Employment equity policy.

Facilitation skills workshops, aimed at library managers, supervisors, librarians and other employees: the value of a wide variety of perspectives in group discussions; seek to have all employees participate in group discussions; specific tools to manage discussions and make decisions.

Intercultural communication, targeted at working with international students.

Intercultural Competence.

Neurodiversity sizism.

Regionalisms (human geography, Appalachian culture), Rites of passage (anthropology).

Religion, Classism/rankism.

Religion, working styles, socio-economic, class distinction in the workplace.

Student veterans, learning styles, gender communication styles.

The answer was "No" above, but there are various trainings and presentations on campus that promote an inclusive workplace.

16. What group/individual is responsible for planning and/or delivering these programs? Check all that apply. N=33

	Plan	Deliver	N
HR/Personnel officer	19	12	21
Diversity Committee or other related group	19	13	19
Staff Development officer	11	6	11
Diversity officer	7	7	9
Multicultural Librarian	3	3	3
Other individual or group	8	12	14
Number of responses	31	27	

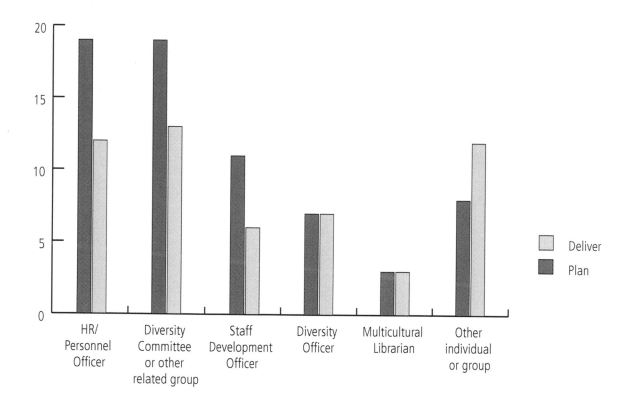

Please briefly describe the other individual or group and their role.

Academic Personnel Librarian serves ex-officio to Diversity Committee to provide guidance and support.

Administrative Director (planning).

Campus Partners: Office of Equal Opportunity and Access; Office of Inclusion and Intercultural Relations; School of Social Work, LGBT Center (delivery).

Campus-level units charged with planning and delivering diversity initiatives.

Coordinator for Services for Persons with Disabilities (delivery).

Delivery is by campus personnel or external presenters.

Director for Administrative Services, Diversity Committee.

Hired consultants or speakers (delivery).

Library administration provides planning and financial support, and actively participates in diversity forums.

One member of our staff, currently involved with the university's staff affairs committee, who developed a program and resource guide relating to physical disabilities (both a relating to co-workers and library users).

Some is planned and delivered out of the president's office, some out of campus Quality Service.

Theuniversity has a number of centralized services with advocacy and support responsibilities.

University HR/Training/Diversity and outside vendors (Cambridge Hill Partners, Global Lead Management Consulting). Library piloted training and materials that later became part of university-wide training curriculum. In addition to Library Diversity Council, we also have a Library Disability Services Committee. University-wide affinity groups have been useful for both recruiting and retention, well received by current and potential staff.

University Office for Equity and Diversity (delivery).

Comments

At this time, we have already offered this program to all our professional staff. We are planning to complete with the rest of our staff, then to repeat the operation and maybe add more parts to our program. We are working with Human Resources Management to develop the program.

Examples of large events: Sign Language Forum, International Party.

Our Diversity Task Force is in a rebuilding phase and will focus on other issues in 2010/11.

Programs are delivered by the university, not specifically through the library.

Since 2004, the library has offered facilitation skills workshops twice yearly on average. The workshops are designed to help library managers, supervisors, librarians and other employees to: seek to include a wide variety of perspectives and opinions in group discussions and decision-making; ensure that everyone participates in group discussions; teach employees how to use specific tools in managing discussions and making decisions.

The deliver piece really depends on the nature of the program. We have turned often to outside experts to deliver programs.

The Staff Development Librarian serves on the Diversity Advisory Committee (DAC) ex-officio. There are programs Staff Development offers that address some of the interests of the DAC and vice versa.

We have a full program of workshops available at the university level through the Office for Equity and Diversity.

17. How many diversity programs for staff does the library typically offer in a year? N=28

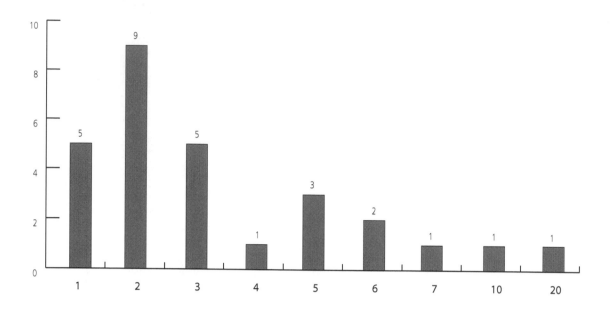

Minimum	Maximum	Mean	Median	Std Dev
1	20	3.79	2.50	3.83

MENTORING PROGRAM

18. Does your library provide a mentoring program specifically to help ethnically/culturally diverse librarians to attain advancement and/or tenure? N=49

Yes	4	8%
No	40	82%
Not yet, but we plan to	5	10%

Comments

Answered Yes

The program we have is specifically designed for the Diversity Resident. All other librarians may participate in the general mentoring program.

Answered Not yet

We hope to create a librarian mentoring program for all newly hired librarians to assist with on-boarding and the promotion process.

Answered No

Formal mentoring program available to all professional staff. Informally, staff from underrepresented groups meet and support each other.

Have existing mentoring program available to all library staff members.

Mentoring is provided to all tenure-track librarians.

Provide a mentoring program for all librarians.

The mentor program is open to all faculty.

Varies by department. No agency-wide program currently exists.

We do have a mentoring program for our librarians, but it is not specifically to help ethnically/culturally diverse librarians.

We have a mentoring program for all new librarians and it is not restricted by ethnicity.

We mentor all probationary librarians as needed and diverse librarians would be included. They are not given different or special treatment.

We offer a mentoring program for all librarians "as they participate in the procedures outlined in the Librarian Personnel Code. The program is designed to support an environment within the University Libraries where librarians can achieve success in their careers and contribute to the overall mission of the University Libraries and the University." (Libraries LAPC charge)

We offering a mentoring program for all new employees, but the focus is on acculturation, not advancement.

EVALUATION AND ASSESSMENT

19. Has your library developed any measures to evaluate the success of efforts to recruit an ethnically/ culturally diverse workforce? N=49

Yes	11	22%
No	29	59%
Not yet, but we plan to	9	18%

If yes, please briefly describe those measures.

Annual diversity report to the University Office of Affirmative Action and Multicultural Programs.

Annual reports on diversity results and reports to Congress.

Campus Affirmative Action Office compiles reports.

Demographic analysis of applicant pool for each open position, demographic analysis of Libraries' workforce.

Each year as part of the campus budget report, each department, including the library is asked to look at hiring practices and recent hires from the last fiscal year, as well as projected hires and goals for the upcoming fiscal year.

Equal Opportunity Plan Annual Report.

Our plan lists several related initiatives and each initiative has outcome measures aligned with it. For example, a winter reception for international students will result in more international students using library services. Many of these outcomes, unfortunately, have not been measured yet.

Review of applicant pools for entry-level positions focus on the LIS program the applicant attended. These programs are compared against reports of minority graduation rates. Our goal is to target schools with statistically significant minority graduation rates; a measure of success would be to receive applications from those schools.

We have measures but again, low self-reporting of ethnicity offsets the measures in place.

We keep precise records of where we advertise each position and the type of response we receive. We are also in Phase II of a multi-year longitudinal study to investigate the efficacy of the current recruitment strategies employed by the Association of Research Libraries. These strategies include advertising job vacancies and soliciting applications from a broad spectrum of applicants, with the purpose of recruiting traditionally underrepresented groups in the academic library workforce.

We note progress in this area as part of our annual review of all Libraries' goals and objectives.

20. Has your library developed any measures to evaluate the success of efforts to retain an ethnically/culturally diverse workforce? N=49

Yes	3	6%
No	35	71%
Not yet, but we plan to	11	22%

If yes or planning to, please briefly describe those measures.

Basic underutilization statistical analyses conducted by the campus HR office.

Demographic analysis of Libraries' workforce, semi-annual analysis of turnover and exit interviews.

Equal Opportunity Plan Annual Report.

Historically we have very low turnover, so our efforts have mostly been directed to recruitment. However, we hope that developing the mentoring program will assist with retention and promotion.

We have had several preliminary discussions about this. At this point we have very few diverse folks to retain.

21. **Has your library assessed the workplace climate? N=48**

Yes	22	46%
No	18	38%
Not yet, but we plan to	8	17%

If yes, which method(s) has the library used? Check all that apply. N=22

Survey developed by the library	12	52%
Survey developed by the parent institution	7	30%
ClimateQUAL™	6	26%
Other method	10	44%

Please describe the other assessment method(s).

As part of university-wide climate survey in 2008.

ClimateQUAL™ is an outgrowth of a U of MD developed climate assessment.

Gallup Climate Surveys.

Survey developed by an external contractor.

Survey developed by consultations but administered within the library. Assessed general climate, not specifically diversity.

Survey developed by the Office of Personnel Management (OPM).

Survey developed by the parent institution, Other; ODLC conducted a High Performing Organization Survey (Ken Blanchard product) at the library in 2007; 2008, 2010 – university-wide Towers Watson (formerly Towers-Perrin) International Survey Research (Global Workforce Study). Both have been used to inform the efforts of the Diversity Council.

The university conducts an annual workplace climate assessment, the PULSE survey. The library receives university-wide and library results.

The University of Florida is preparing full-fledged Diversity Plan which will include a workplace climate survey.

Two climate surveys were administered to the Libraries employees in the spring of 2007. The MROC Climate Survey was the first survey, created by the Libraries' Millennium Report Oversight Committee (MROC) but conducted by the university's Office of Institutional Research and Evaluation (OIRE) for the MROC. The second survey given was the Organizational Climate and Diversity Assessment (OCDA), a library climate survey developed by the University of Maryland Libraries to pilot with five academic libraries as a standardized instrument which could measure the "healthiness" of an organization. The OCDA was developed to collect information concerning employee "perceptions of how well the libraries were doing in achieving a healthy organization climate along the principles of diversity."

22. Has your library used the results of these or any other assessment efforts to change the diversity plan and/or diversity programs? N=44

Yes	14	32%
No	22	50%
Not yet, but we plan to	8	18%

Additional comments about assessment.

Answered Yes

Diversity Council submitted recommendations and proposed goals to the Library Executive Committee in September 2009.

Future assessment will be used to make adjustments to the plan and training.

Held a year-long diversity video and discussion series in response to climate survey results.

One concern revealed by our most recent survey was the impact on gender and salary due to recent retirements. This 'reveal' will be used to inform hiring practices and salary reviews.

Specific plans are developed by departments and/or units to address climate issues.

Surveys show significant acceptance of the Libraries' diversity initiatives and indicate that we have an open, welcoming climate. Libraries' Administration works with the Diversity Committee to focus on survey results that indicate concerns or areas needing further work.

Answered Not yet

Plans to implement an assessment tool in winter, 2010. The diversity committee is currently considering ClimateQUAL™ or a survey developed by a peer institution.

We are just to start the implementation phase of the recommendations that were made by the library committee that reviewed and worked to understand our ClimateQUAL™ results.

We plan on holding a series of focus group meetings this summer with our staff to assess what programs/initiatives we should consider in our programming efforts that will enhance the inclusiveness and diversity of our culture.

Answered No

The library has not assessed the workplace climate, however, the university does via a survey developed by the university.

While the library has not performed any assessments, the university has.

23. Please enter any additional information about your library's efforts to recruit and retain a diversity workforce that may assist the authors in accurately analyzing the results of this survey.

All of our job ads have the following statement: The University of Alberta hires on the basis of merit. We are committed to the principle of equity in employment. We welcome diversity and encourage applications from all qualified women and men, including persons with disabilities, members of visible minorities, and Aboriginal persons.

Campus diversity resource office and dean of students office provide 20–25 programs per year dealing with race and ethnicity, sexual orientation, gender and/or age discrimination, physical disabilities, language barriers, religion, and other aspects of diversity. Library encourages staff participation by providing information, release time, and fees (if any).

From the University Employment Equity Web site: The University conducts a self-identification survey. Aggregate results are provided to the Employment Equity Officer, so they may identify gaps in representation. Qualitative data is gathered from the under-represented groups to ascertain what factors are linked to under representation. Plans are then created in partnership with unions and management to close identified gaps in representation.

Many of our librarians participate in the university-wide minority mentoring program. Though this is not specifically a library program it is a program supported by the Dean of Libraries.

Oklahoma State University has an excellent Institutional Diversity department. We use their program, policies, etc. within the library.

The Library Diversity Committee Web page is not available to the public so it is not possible to share program information related to diversity.

The library is seen as a leader in diversity and inclusion efforts for systemic changes across Yale's campus. The Library Diversity Council partners closely with the Chief Diversity Officer, Human Resources, and Yale's affinity groups for staff members. While the current economic/budget climate has limited funding for some outreach activities, we do see a growing pipeline of diversity candidates in library school and early career demographics.

The Library of Congress has recently established a redesigned Office of Inclusiveness and Compliance (OIC), which has responsibility for oversight of this issue and related functions.

The University has recently approved the Aboriginal strategic plan to coincide with the University strategic plan. The following may be applicable: Educator's toolbook: Global Citizenship: an educator's toolbook http://www.gc.tag.ubc. ca/

The University Library recruits librarians from diverse backgrounds through a Targeted Opportunity Program (TOPS), which is a program run by the Provost's Office. The University Library also supports the LIS Access Midwest Program (LAMP), an IMLS funded recruitment program by offering a paid-internship to one of the LAMP scholars each summer. The Outreach Librarian for Multicultural Services also serves on the LAMP organizing committee.

We are currently accepting applications for an Academic Librarian Diversity Internship. This is the culmination of several years of work to put something like this in place.

We have recently joined the LAMP program (LIS Access Midwest Program), and will be offering an Undergraduate Minority Internship opportunity this summer. We hope to host two interns a year.

RESPONDING INSTITUTIONS

University at Albany, SUNY

University of Alberta

University of Arizona

Brigham Young University

University of British Columbia

University at Buffalo, SUNY

University of Calgary

University of California, Irvine

University of California, Los Angeles

University of California, Riverside

University of California, Santa Barbara

University of Delaware

University of Florida

George Washington University

University of Georgia

University of Illinois at Urbana-Champaign

University of Iowa

Iowa State University

Kent State University

Library of Congress

University of Louisville

McGill University

McMaster University

University of Manitoba

University of Maryland

University of Massachusetts Amherst

University of Miami

University of Minnesota

University of Missouri

Université de Montréal

University of Nebraska–Lincoln

University of North Carolina at Chapel Hill

North Carolina State University

Northwestern University

Ohio University

Oklahoma State University

Pennsylvania State University

Purdue University

Rice University

University of Rochester

Rutgers University

Syracuse University

Texas Tech University

Virginia Tech

University of Washington

Washington University in St. Louis

University of Waterloo

Yale University

York University

REPRESENTATIVE DOCUMENTS

Diversity Statements

UNC HOME | LIBRARIES, COLLECTIONS & HOURS | E-RESEARCH TOOLS | E-JOURNAL FINDER | CATALOG

UNC
UNIVERSITY LIBRARIES

ABOUT THE LIBRARIES

Diversity Statement

The University Library affirms the University's core values with respect to diversity. We strive to create an environment in which students, faculty, and staff who differ, for example, in social backgrounds, economic circumstances, personal characteristics, philosophical outlooks, life experiences, perspectives, beliefs, expectations, and aspirations feel welcomed and respected.

As we seek to foster a library culture that is supportive of diversity, we commit to:

- Treat coworkers and library users the way we want to be treated, being mindful to respect difference.
- Work together cooperatively for the good of the Library, basing discussion on facts rather than rumor, stereotypes, or assumptions about others.
- Ensure that library staff, services, and collections reflect the diversity of the UNC community and the world.

Working and learning in this environment enhances the experience for everyone.

Home | Hours | Search This Site | UNC Home

Website comments or questions: Library Web Team
Suggestions on Library Services? Give us your feedback.
URL: http://www.lib.unc.edu/about/diversity.html
This page was last updated Wednesday, July 29, 2009.

ALICE | InfoTree | FAQ | home

ASK A LIBRARIAN ▶
im | chat | phone | e-mail | skype | appointment

| Find | Services | Collections | Library Info |

Culture Showcase Home Page

Current theme:

International Student

Experience at Ohio U.

  Speakers

  Bibliography

Previous themes:

  American Regionalisms

  Appalachian Women

  African American

   Heritage

  African American Studies

   & Alden Library

  Celebrating Firsts

  Presidential Politics

  Rites of Passage

Libraries' Diversity Program

Diversity Committee

The Libraries' Diversity Program

Mission

Recognizing that all people have individual differences and are the product of one or more cultures and ethnic backgrounds, Ohio University Libraries is committed to cultivating an environment where differences are valued and respected. The Libraries strive to provide an inclusive environment for all individuals regardless of race, religion, ethnicity, background, gender, and disability and will actively promote and support diversity among our administrators, faculty, staff, and students.

We seek to do the following:

1. Address the information needs of all library patrons, taking individual needs into account;
2. Build collections representing diverse viewpoints and opinions and expressions, regardless of format;
3. Produce culturally stimulating programs and services that enhance the academic experience of the University community;
4. Improve the diversity of the Libraries staff.

Archives & Special Collections | Fine Arts | Government Documents | International Collections | Music & Dance

OHIO University Libraries
Athens, OH 45701-2978
Phone: (740) 593-2699

Last updated: April 23, 2010
This page is maintained by the Diversity Committee.
Please use our Feedback Form for your questions, comments, and suggestions about the Libraries' services and resources.

PENNSTATE
UNIVERSITY | LIBRARIES

Diversity

Penn State University Libraries Definition of Diversity:

The University Libraries provide The Pennsylvania State University communities with equitable access to all of its information resources and services.

This access is guaranteed without regard to race, ethnicity, language, age, religion or spiritual beliefs, health, gender, sexual orientation, physical capabilities, or geographic origin.

The University Libraries are committed to providing equal access to employment and opportunity for advancement without regard to personal characteristics not related to ability, performance or qualifications as determined by University policy or by state and federal authorities.

One of the most succinct statements about the University's diversity objectives is contained in a presentation by former Provost of Penn State, John Brighton, to the University Board of Trustees in 1993. Under the topic "What Do We Mean By Diversity," Provost Brighton provided several descriptors:

- Reasonable representation from different minority groups
- Representation from different countries and cultures
- Reasonable balance of gender
- Diversity in curriculum content
- Climate supportive of different minority groups and cultures

This conception of diversity provides a viable foundation for official efforts to describe the University's diversity objectives . . . ." These two definitions together comprise the Libraries' working definitions of diversity.

Fostering Diversity in the University Libraries

A Framework to Foster Diversity at Penn State University Libraries
Strategic Plan 2004-2009

University Libraries 2004-09 Diversity Framework- Final Report

University Libraries 2010-15 Diversity Strategic Plan

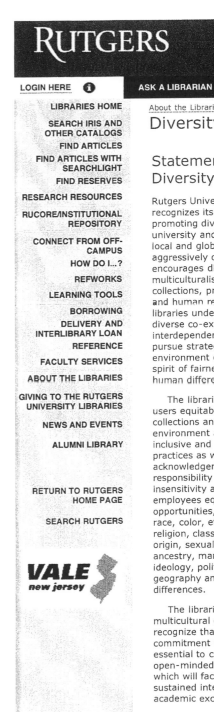

About the Libraries:

Diversity Resources

Statement on Diversity

Rutgers University Libraries recognizes its exceptional role in promoting diversity within the university and its surrounding local and global community. It aggressively cultivates and encourages diversity and multiculturalism through its collections, programs, services and human resources. The libraries understand the value of diverse co-existence and interdependence and actively pursue strategies to achieve an environment of respect and a spirit of fairness and tolerance for human differences.

The libraries ensure all its users equitable access to its collections and services. Its work environment and ethic reflects inclusive and participatory practices as well as an acknowledgement of responsibility for preventing bias, insensitivity and ensuring all its employees equal access to opportunities, without regard to race, color, ethnicity, sex, religion, class, disability, national origin, sexual orientation, ancestry, marital status, culture, ideology, politics, income, geography and regional differences.

The libraries are proud to be a multicultural community and recognize that a strong commitment to diversity is essential to creating a fair and open-minded work environment which will facilitate unique and sustained intellectual and academic excellence.

- **Table of Contents**
  - Rutgers University

(© iStockphoto/MaleWitch)

"We all should know that diversity makes for a rich tapestry, and we must understand that all the threads of the tapestry are equal in value no matter what their color."
- Maya Angelou

Diversity Plans

Library Committee Handbook

-- Index of Committees
-- Planning Calendar

Diversity Committee

Committee Charge

Agendas and Minutes

Diversity Goals 2007-2012

Diversity and Multicultural Information

_____

E-mail:
diversity@library.uiuc.edu

Library » Committees » Library Diversity Committee » University Library Diversity Goals 2007-2012

University Library Diversity Goals 2007-2012

Goals

1. Create a welcoming environment for all members of the community.
   Strategies
   - Increase awareness and understanding of diversity among Library employees, including students, by:

     i. Providing training, workshops, and other educational opportunities, and incorporating diversity training into existing training opportunities (e.g., training for graduate assistants and student assistants). Training should focus both on general concepts and values and on issues relating to providing service and content to a diverse community;

     ii. Developing mentoring programs for all new librarians and staff so that they better understand the Library's culture;

     iii. Holding forums and discussions that feature participants from diverse communities that would allow employees to ask questions and improve their knowledge of other cultures, backgrounds, and people with disabilities;

     iv. Promoting the understanding that diversity is a celebration of differences and identification of similarities;

     v. Collaborating with other campus-level groups with similar missions (e.g., CITES) and

     vi. Improving the website overseen by the Diversity Committee so that it will serve as the hub of useful information for employees.

   Who's Responsible
   - Library administration
   - Diversity Committee
   - All employees

2. Enhance teaching, learning and research by improving access to information resources that serve the needs of a diverse academic community.

   Strategies
   - Expand purchase of resources that represent the experience of diverse and underrepresented communities;
   - Move towards meeting 100% of accessibility standards in all Library web pages;

- Collaborate with DRES to work with content providers to make their materials accessible;
- Have an always up-to-date Gateway that provides easy access across disciplines and cultures;
- Form collaborations with groups that serve under-served communities (e.g., OLLI) and that produce or distribute content for under-served populations;
- Create websites, exhibits, and publications that highlight the Library's resources on diversity; and
- Work with consortial partners to expand awareness of vendors about accessibility issues for purchased or licensed information resources.

Who's Responsible

- Associate University Librarians

3. Recruit and retain faculty from diverse cultures and races and with disabilities that reflect societal demographics.

Strategies

- Continue to seek candidates for TOP hires;
- Improve recruitment strategies to build the most diverse pools possible;
- Participate in and support regional and national programs that recruit minority students to the profession (e.g., LAMP: LIS Access Midwest Program; ARL Initiative to Recruit a Diverse Workforce); and
- Support participation of individual library faculty in ARL's Leadership & Career Development Program

Who's Responsible

- University Librarian

University Library
University of Illinois at Urbana-Champaign
1408 W. Gregory Dr. | Urbana, IL 61801
217-333-2290

For comments on this page contact: Gateway Conversion

Last modified by: Anna Dombrowski on 5/8/08

**University Libraries
Strategic Diversity Implementation
Plan 2006-2010**

Dean Mark Weber

	Diversity Initiative/Action	Strategic Theme/Goal & Objective	Outcome Measures	Timeline
1.	When appropriate make purchases though diverse suppliers registered at KSU.	Theme: One University with a Diverse Community. Objective 5. Increase the participation of minority and women owned businesses by implementing Kent State's supplier diversity plan.	i. An increase in purchase orders executed with diverse vendors.	Implement by 5/2008. Review progress annually.
	Contact Person: Emily Hermon **Budget:** No additional funding **New or Continuing:** New			
2.	Update "Minority Recruitment Resources Guide" and renew efforts to list open positions in diverse markets.	Theme: One University with a Diverse Community. Objective 2. Increase the number of underrepresented faculty in all academic programs. Objective 4. Increase the number of underrepresented staff and administrators at all levels of the university.	i. An increase in the number of diverse applicants for LMS positions.	Document updated by 1/2008. The document will be reviewed and updated biannually.
	Contact Person: Ken Burhanna (document), Emily Hermon (implementation) **Budget:** No additional funding **New or Continuing:** Continuing			

Macintosh HD:Users:leeanne:Dropbox:DATA:Lee Anne Data:SPEC:319 Diversity Plans:DPP Docs:LMS Diversity Implementation Plan - Revised - Fall 2008.doc

1

	Diversity Initiative/Action	Strategic Theme/Goal & Objective	Outcome Measures	Timeline
3.	Instructional outreach to KSU feeder high schools, inviting classes of students to visit the university and library and giving them academic experiences that prepare them for college and potentially KSU.	Theme: One University with a Diverse Community. Objective 1. Increase the number of underrepresented students in each academic program and recognized student organizations.	i. An increase in number students attending KSU from these high schools. ii. An improvement in the success and persistence of incoming KSU students from these high schools.	Program data reviewed each summer.
		Theme: One University with Equitable Retention Objective 2. Integrate and link support services provided for racially, ethnically diverse students as well as gay and lesbian students, students with disabilities and students from diverse religious backgrounds.		
	Notes: Future strategy that may be added will be to target local high schools with large populations of underrepresented students and work with them. Program is formally called "Informed Transitions" www.library.kent.edu/highschool. It has been in place since fall 2004. Over 1500 students have visited since its inception.			
	Contact Person: Ken Burhanna **Budget:** No additional funding **New or Continuing:** Continuing			
4.	Review and improve faculty/staff mentoring program by: - surveying current faculty - consulting with Dr. Michael	Theme: One University with Equitable Retention Objective 3. Develop individualized retention programs for underrepresented faculty members and staff through the Vice Provost.	i. Faculty will persist and progress at a high rate. ii. Improvements and/or revisions will be identified and made to the mentoring program.	Survey faculty by 5/2008. Consult with Dr. Michael by 12/2008. Revise/update mentoring program by 5/2009.
		Theme: One University with Equitable Progress for All Objective 1. Identify and eliminate institutional obstacles that may impede the progress of women and underrepresented faculty.		
	Contact Persons: Faculty Professional Development Committee (within LMS) **Budget:** No additional funding required at this time. **New or Continuing:** Continuing			

Macintosh HD:Users:leeanne:Dropbox:DATA:Lee Anne Data:SPEC:319 Diversity Plans:DPP Docs:LMS Diversity Implementation Plan - Revised - Fall 2008.doc

2

	Diversity Initiative/Action	Strategic Theme/Goal & Objective	Outcome Measures	Timeline
5.	Engage the university community in diversity by sponsoring programs and inviting lecturers to speak during Black History Month.	Theme: One University with Opportunities for Diversity Leadership Objective 3. Encourage Kent State leadership in the community, region, state and nation on matters concerning diversity. Objective 5. Provide resources that will enable Kent State to offer ongoing diversity training for a wide range of audiences. Theme: One University Embracing All Diversity Competencies Objective 6. Promote a rich educational environment that provides in-classroom and out-of-classroom opportunities for students to interact, experience, and grow in all aspects of diversity.	i. The scheduling of a speaker for 2008. ii. Seeking an attendance of 30 or more KSU community members.	Program data reviewed each summer.
	Notes: Program has existed for a number of years. Past speakers include: Bob Moses (2004), William A. Allen (2005), Peter N. Kirsanow (2006), and Lee H. Walker (2007).			
	Contact Person: Mark Weber **Budget:** $7,000 set aside **New or Continuing:** Continuing			
6.	Instructional outreach to diverse and underserved groups to ensure they feel welcome at the library and have the skills necessary to succeed.	Theme: One University with Equitable Retention Objective 2. Integrate and link support services provided for racially, ethnically diverse students as well as gay and lesbian students, students with disabilities and students from diverse religious backgrounds. Theme: One University with a Welcoming Environment Objective 3. Improve awareness of and services to underrepresented students.	i. Students having instructional experiences with the library will persist at a higher rate. ii. Students having instructional experiences with the library will take advantage of library services and resources at a high rate.	Instructional efforts are reviewed annually. Plan on conducting more intensive assessment projects during 2008-2009.
	Contact Person: Ken Burhanna and Mary Lee Jensen **Budget:** No additional funding required **New or Continuing:** Continuing	**Notes:** Groups include Academic STARS, GED Scholars, Science Learning Community, International Students, Graduate Students of Color, and Adult Student Orientation.		

Macintosh HD:Users:leeanne.Dropbox:DATA:Lee Anne Data:SPEC:319 Diversity Plans:DPP Docs:LMS Diversity Implementation Plan - Revised - Fall 2008.doc

3

54 · Representative Documents: Diversity Plans

	Diversity Initiative/Action	Strategic Theme/Goal & Objective	Outcome Measures	Timeline
7.	Increase the development of collections that support diversity and its research by offering diversity collection development grants to faculty.	Theme: One University Embracing All Diversity Competencies Objective 4. Support active research on diversity issues, preparation of research papers, and publication of findings.	i. Increase in the number and quality of research collections related to diversity issues.	Review possible grant program by 5/2008. (Tentative) Put out call for grant applications in spring 2009. (Tentative) Begin awarding grants and acquiring collections during 2009-2010.
		Objective 5. Organize a support system for faculty who teach diversity courses and faculty who wish to broaden their knowledge and skills of cross-cultural pedagogy.		
		Theme: One University with Opportunities for Diversity Leadership Objective 5. Provide resources that will enable Kent State to offer ongoing diversity training for a wide range of audiences.		
	Contact Person: Mark Weber **Budget:** $3,000 **New or Continuing:** New	**Notes:**		
8.	Annual professional development session for faculty and staff devoted to diversity issues.	Theme: One University Embracing All Diversity Competencies Objective 5. Organize a support system for faculty who teach diversity courses and faculty who wish to broaden their knowledge and skills of cross-cultural pedagogy.	i. Faculty and staff will develop and improve professional competencies related to diversity.	Professional development programming is reviewed annually.
		Theme: One University with a Welcoming Environment Objective 5. Provide team-building as well as diversity awareness workshops for staff, faculty and administrators.		
	Contact Person: Paul Fehrmann **Budget:** $1,000 **New or Continuing:** New	**Notes:** First session was conducted last summer: "Teaching Across Cultures" was presented by Charles Nieman.		

Macintosh HD:Users:leeanne.Dropbox:DATA:Lee Anne Data:SPEC:319 Diversity Plans:DPP Docs:LMS Diversity Implementation Plan - Revised - Fall 2008.doc

4

#	Diversity Initiative/Action	Strategic Theme/Goal & Objective	Outcome Measures	Timeline
9.	LMS faculty members make ongoing contributions to diversity as a professional issue within librarianship at the state and/or national level by providing leadership within the Academic Library Association of Ohio (ALAO) and the American Library Association (ALA).	Theme: One University with Opportunities for Diversity Leadership Objective 3. Encourage Kent State leadership in the community, region, state and nation on matters concerning diversity.	i. Vice Provost Dr. Steve Michael will provide a keynote address to the Diversity Workshop during the 2007 ALAO Conference in Columbus, Ohio. ii. UDAC representative Ken Burhanna will be attending the National Diversity in Libraries Conference in 2008. iii. Ken Burhanna may seek to chair the ALAO Diversity Committee in 2008. He is currently a committee member.	ALAO Conference in 2007. Increased leadership opportunities possible in 2008–2009.
	Contact Person: Ken Burhanna **Budget:** Existing travel budget **New or Continuing:** New	**Notes:**		
10.	Staff Recognition Luncheon and Student Worker Appreciation Luncheon	Theme: One University with Equitable Progress for All Objective 3. Monitor the reward and recognition programs of the university to ensure that no group is disadvantaged because of race, age, gender, religion, disability, nationality, ideological or sexual orientation.	i. Faculty and staff will make equitable progress and be rewarded equally for their contributions. ii. Student workers will feel appreciated, have high morale and will be retained from year to year.	Both luncheons occur annually during the spring semester.
	Contact Person: Mark Weber, Pamela Lemmons, Mary Lovin **Budget:** $1,000 **New or Continuing:** Continuing	**Notes:**		

Macintosh HD:Users:leeanne.Dropbox:DATA:Lee Anne Data:SPEC:319 Diversity Plans:DPP Docs:LMS Diversity Implementation Plan - Revised - Fall 2008.doc

5

56 · Representative Documents: Diversity Plans

	Diversity Initiative/Action	Strategic Theme/Goal & Objective	Outcome Measures	Timeline
11.	Provide student workspaces and resources that are diverse and supportive and welcoming in the library. This is a large initiative that has been underway for some time. It concludes the development of the Information Commons on the 1st floor of the Main Library, the provision of Math and Writing Tutoring, the development of the Student Multimedia Studio, the renovation of quiet and group student spaces. The newest piece will involve the *Writing Center* moving into the library (cost to library $50,000).	Theme: One University with a Welcoming Environment Objective. Provide quality physical and social environments for students and employees of all backgrounds. Theme: One University with Equitable Progress for All Objective 4. Adopt programs informed by data to enhance graduation rates of underrepresented students. Theme: One University with Equitable Retention Objective 2. Integrate and link support services.....	(Near term measures) i. At its new location, the Writing Center will equal and surpass tutoring hours provided. ii. LMS will experience increased referrals from the Writing Center to other services available at the library. (Long term measure) iii. Students who have experiences with library support services will persist at a higher rate.	Writing Center should be operational within the library by fall 2007. Library spaces and their uses are reviewed on an ongoing basis.
	Contact Person: Barbara Schloman **Budget:** $50,000 **New or Continuing:** Continuing	**Notes:** The Writing Center move and partnership is a collaboration between LMS and the English Department.		
12.	International Student Winter Reception Librarians and staff invite international students to the library for a mid-day reception. Snacks, refreshments and library tours are offered.	Theme: One University with a Welcoming Environment Objective 3. Improve awareness of and services to underrepresented students. Theme: One University with Equitable Retention Objective 2. Integrate and link support services.	i. Participation in the reception will increase the participation of international students in library programming. ii. Experiences will reveal future opportunities for supporting international students and understanding their needs.	Reception is planned at the end of each fall semester and scheduled for the intersession preceding the spring semester.
	Contact Person: Tammy Voelker **Budget:** $500 **New or Continuing:** New	**Notes:** First reception occurred this past January during intersession.		

Macintosh HD:Users:leeanne:Dropbox:DATA:Lee Anne Data:SPEC:319 Diversity Plans:DPP Docs:LMS Diversity Implementation Plan - Revised - Fall 2008.doc

	Diversity Initiative/Action	Strategic Theme/Goal & Objective	Outcome Measures	Timeline
13.	Annual Information Commons Open House New students are welcomed to the libraries. Refreshments, snacks and library tours are offered. Games and give-a-ways are used to increase student engagement.	Theme: One University with a Welcoming Environment Objective 3. Improve awareness of and services to underrepresented students.	i. Equal or surpass the number of students who attend the Open House from the preceding year. In 2006 over 400 students attended.	The Open House is held on the Friday of Week of Welcome.
		Theme: One University with Equitable Retention Objective 2. Integrate and link support services.	ii. Equal or surpass the number of students who take library tours that day (365 in 2006).	
	Contact Person: Ken Burhanna **Budget:** $1000 **New or Continuing:** New	**Notes:** This is a Week of Welcome initiative.		
14.	Career awareness outreach to Exploratory, BUS and Latino undergraduate student organizations to promote librarianship.	Theme: One University with a Diverse Community Objective 2. Increase the number of underrepresented faculty in all academic programs.	i.Increase the number of students who pursue graduate study in librarianship.	Initiative is at very early stages. Plan on piloting an outreach program by 2008-2009.
			ii. Increase the number of librarians in the field from diverse backgrounds.	
	Contact Person: Mark Weber and Ken Burhanna **Budget:** No additional funding required **New or Continuing:** New	**Notes:** Because the profession of librarianship has so few candidates from diverse backgrounds, these types of "grow your own" programs are necessary.		

Macintosh HD:Users:leeanne:Dropbox:DATA:Lee Anne Data:SPEC:319 Diversity Plans:DPP Docs:LMS Diversity Implementation Plan - Revised - Fall 2008.doc

7

#	Diversity Initiative/Action	Strategic Theme/Goal & Objective	Outcome Measures	Timeline
15.	Establish a partnership with historically black universities. These partnerships would attract graduating seniors at these institutions to enroll at the School of Library and Information Science at KSU and work under an assistantship for Libraries and Media Services. Partnerships with Lincoln University and Central State University have yet to result in a partnership agreement, but we plan to continue pursuing this. **Contact Person:** Mark Weber **Budget:** Pending, uncertain at this point. **New or Continuing:** Continuing	Theme: One University with a Diverse Community Objective 2. Increase the number of underrepresented faculty in all academic programs.	i. Create a partnership with one or more of these historically black universities by 2010.	This initiative is reviewed annually.
		Notes: This has been explored as a partnership with the School of Library and Information Science.		

#	Diversity Initiative/Action	Strategic Theme/Goal & Objective	Outcome Measures	Timeline
16.	Make strong commitment to diversity by including it in the revision of Libraries and Media Services' mission statement **Contact Person:** Mark Weber **Budget:** None **New or Continuing:** New	Theme: One University with a Diverse Community Objective 2. Increase the number of underrepresented faculty in all academic programs.	i. Release new mission statement that recognizes diversity as an important value.	Finish by end of 2008-2009 academic year.
		Notes:		

Macintosh HD:Users:leeanne:Dropbox:DATA:Lee Anne Data:SPEC:319 Diversity Plans:DPP Docs:LMS Diversity Implementation Plan - Revised - Fall 2008.doc

8

	Diversity Initiative/Action	Strategic Theme/Goal & Objective	Outcome Measures	Timeline
		Theme: One University with a Diverse Community	i. Establish a committee with a charge that is codified in the faculty handbook.	This initiative is reviewed annually.
17.	Establish a diversity committee comprised of faculty, staff and students that will oversee and coordinate diversity initiatives and help articulate this implementation plan.	Objective 2. Increase the number of underrepresented faculty in all academic programs.		
	Contact Person: Mark Weber **Budget:** None **New or Continuing:** New	**Notes:**		

Macintosh HD:Users:leeanne.Dropbox:DATA:Lee Anne Data:SPEC:319 Diversity Plans:DPP Docs:LMS Diversity Implementation Plan - Revised - Fall 2008.doc

9

University of Louisville
2008-2010 Unit Diversity Plan Template
(REVISED 11/08)

Unit:_ U of L Libraries

Vision Statement:

▶ **Vision Statement:**

Mission:
The University of Louisville Libraries fosters a welcoming environment inclusive in its understanding and integration of the dimensions of diversity, including, but not limited to diversity based on race and ethnicity, gender, disability, sexual orientation, age, religion, and class.
The University Libraries are charged with two fundamental goals: 1) to encourage the recruitment and hiring of employees who represent the diversity of our society, at all levels, including professional, paraprofessional, and student assistants; and 2) to use our collections and programs to enhance the understanding of the kaleidoscope of diversity.

Goals:
The specific objectives for the Libraries Diversity Task Force are to:
- Regularly monitor and update diversity plan to ensure the Libraries are in line with the diversity goals of the University
- Monitor diversity climate to determine the needs, concerns, and perceptions of Libraries faculty, staff, and students
- Use appropriate outlets to communicate and promote diversity goals and efforts
- Partner with others to provide educational, inspirational, and transformative diversity programs

Diversity Scorecard Goals: Advance diversity through the <u>workforce</u>, <u>student populations</u>, <u>programs and training</u> (measurements for unit scorecards.

Goals	Diversity Category	Strategies	Tactics/Action	Assessment / Measurement	Timeline
Increase enrollment, retention and graduation rates of students of color (undergraduate, graduate and professional)	Students	Partner with academic units and student groups to provide academic support to students of color	Participate in programs/events offered by the cultural center to promote library services		Outreach to cultural center began in 2008
			Provide library instruction for international students	Increase awareness of library services and usage by international students	Library orientation session offered in

Set to Print Landscape on Legal Paper

	Employees				2008
Increase employment and retention of faculty, staff and administrators of color (full time)		Maintain or increase the number of faculty, staff, and administrators of color and underrepresented groups	Meet with diverse student groups (such as the Porter Scholars) to create awareness of library services available	Increase in library research sessions and usage by Porter Scholars students	Diversity Resident Librarian will hold introduction to the library class for Porter Scholars in fall 2009
		Work towards increasing the diversity of applicant pools	Promote open library positions in publications, lists, and at events that target minority applicants	Percentage of increase of applicants	This is a standard and ongoing process for advertising open positions
			Request data from HR on previous applicant pools to determine diversity of applicants		
		Retain staff, faculty, and administrators	Provide mentoring, professional development opportunities, and reward/ recognize the work of staff, faculty, and administrators	Percentage of staff and faculty of color retained	Mentoring program for tenure track faculty created in 2008. Program is ongoing.
					Mentoring is also a component of the diversity residency program
			Conduct a satisfaction survey of current faculty and staff of color to measure the effectiveness of retention efforts	Percentage of favorable results from faculty, staff, and administrators.	

Set to Print Landscape on Legal Paper

2

	Programs and Training			
Increase number of programs related to diversity education, networking opportunities and training.	Continue to partner with other units to provide diversity training and educational programs for staff, faculty and students	Create evaluation process to determine success of programs, and gage interest and needs of participants Use evaluation data to determine future programs	Maintain high level of diversity programming.	Evaluation form and processes to be completed in 2009
	Continue to provide a welcoming and efficient space for diversity related events to be used by the University community	Review room reservation calendars to determine how the spaces are being used, by whom, type of events, etc. Contact a sampling to gage satisfaction. Insure policies and processes for using space in the libraries are straightforward and easy to follow	Maintain high level of use of space for diversity related events by the University community	Diversity Task Force will conduct a review of usage data in 2009

Set to Print Landscape on Legal Paper

3

Strategic Plan 2020 Theme: DIVERSITY, OPPORTUNITY & SOCIAL JUSTICE

University Theme: Actively welcome all to a center of learning that embraces the diversity of ideas, cultures and people

▶ The University Libraries strives to create a welcoming, inclusive environment for students, employees, and community that serves as a center of learning where diversity is celebrated through collections, exhibits, and programming.

Goals	Diversity Category	Strategies	Tactics/Action	Assessment / Measurement	Timeline
Implement programs to assist minorities and women to become academic and university leaders					
Recruit and hire underrepresented people of color and women for leadership positions	Leadership Employees	Maintain or increase number of women and librarians of color	Advertise administrative and librarian positions in all appropriate lists for librarians from underrepresented groups	In 2008, 2 of the 4 open faculty positions were filled by women from under-represented groups, one at the management level	Efforts are ongoing, as positions become available
			Network and publicize positions at local, regional, and national library meetings		

Set to Print Landscape on Legal Paper

4

Implement programs that provide mentoring and internship opportunities for development of internal underrepresented people of color and women as leaders	Leadership Employees Students	Provide opportunities for librarians from underrepresented groups to gain leadership experiences		In 2008 a librarian received funding to attend the Minnesota Institute for New Librarians of Color, a weeklong leadership institute. Libraries plan to send other employees to Institute in the future
		Provide funds for librarians to attend leadership conferences and institutes	Increased knowledge and preparation for leadership within the profession	A recently hired librarian was accepted into the American Library Association (ALA) Emerging Leader's program and will attend conferences in 2009
				Program kickoff was held in 2008
			The Libraries' mentoring program has been restructured and is available for probationary faculty who are preparing for tenure	

Set to Print Landscape on Legal Paper

5

Goals	Diversity Category	Strategies	Tactics/Action	Assessment / Measurement	Timeline
Develop a campus environment that is welcoming to all people and in which diversity, social justice and provision of academic opportunity are intrinsic values					
Incorporate principles of cultural diversity, global awareness and social justice into appropriate portions of educational curricula, research and scholarship programs and programs in civic engagement	Leadership Curriculum Employees Students	Contribute to student awareness of other cultures, global awareness, and social justice issues through programming and exhibits within the libraries	Host yearly events/exhibits that highlight diversity Sponsor yearly exhibits/events featuring African American history or authors Offer programs and exhibits that educate and create discussion around issues of social justice and global awareness	Review of program evaluations from participants	Programs offered throughout the year
Implement a review of the Americans with Disabilities Act review and prepare a unit action plan	Leadership Employees Students	Ensure Libraries are equipped to serve needs of students and employees with disabilities, with regard to physical accommodations, services, and accessibility.	Implement a review of Libraries Website to identify ways to improve accessibility for patrons with disabilities Devise a plan to make improvements	Use available software to assess Libraries web pages to determine compliance with ADA requirements	In process
Support student learning on issues of diversity, social justice, and global awareness through the library collections		Ensure library collections reflect campus diversity	Regularly monitor holdings and approval plans to ensure the Libraries are purchasing books, films, and electronic/digital resources that support areas of study at the University, and are inclusive of diversity, social justice, and global awareness The University Archives and Special Collections areas are committed to providing widespread access to diverse materials, and recently launched a digital collection of its African American oral histories	Review of collection growth data	Ongoing process

Set to Print Landscape on Legal Paper

6

Goals	Diversity Category	Strategies	Tactics/Action	Assessment / Measurement	Timeline
Identify ways to communicate diversity efforts to the campus community		Communicate diversity efforts to campus community Improve participation and support for diversity events and programs sponsored by the libraries	Promote diversity efforts through the Libraries diversity program page Promote Libraries events & programs through appropriate campus news organs Ensure library subject pages list and link to diversity resources and collections	Percentage of increase in program participation/support	Ongoing
Partner with other campus units to provide an inclusive, diverse, engaging, learning environment	Leadership Employees Students	Create a learning environment where students are welcomed and issues of diversity and social justice are embraced and promoted	Provide office space for the Muhammad Ali Institute for Peace and Justice Provide space for the Anne Braden Institute for Social Justice Research	Completion of areas in the libraries for these offices	Done

Increase diversity within the field of library science

Goals	Diversity Category	Strategies	Tactics/Action	Assessment / Measurement	Timeline
Increase diversity within the profession including minorities from underrepresented groups					
Provide professional library experiences through internships and residencies for MLS students/recent graduates from underrepresented groups	Leadership Employees	Prepare library science students and recent graduates from underrepresented groups for careers in library science Increase diversity in the profession and the U of L Libraries	Since the inception of the program, 3 librarian interns (2 African Americans and 1 Hispanic) from underrepresented groups have graduated with MLS degrees and have been promoted to librarian positions The Libraries also hired an African American male resident for the 2006-2007 school year The libraries formalized its Diversity Residency Program to provide a 2-3 year residency for a new librarian from an underrepresented group. The search process was completed in spring of 2008.	Increase in the number of librarians from underrepresented groups in academic librarian positions Increase in the number of minorities within the profession of library science	New library resident began in summer of 2008

Set to Print Landscape on Legal Paper

7

	Students	Increase interest in the field of library science and number of applicants to LIS programs	Contact minority student groups and organizations on the UofL campuses about professional opportunities in librarianship	Increased awareness of library science programs, scholarships, library positions, and related information	Ongoing
Promote the field of librarianship to increase interest for students from underrepresented groups			Contact local volunteer, community outreach, and pre-professional minority organizations about professional opportunities in librarianship		
			Speak to local school groups about the profession and expose them to the field		
			Provide student assistants with information about the field of library science		

Set to Print Landscape on Legal Paper

Implement strategies to retain minority hires

Goals	Diversity Category	Strategies	Tactics/Action	Assessment / Measurement	Timeline
Develop programs and initiatives that contribute to the professional growth and success of minority faculty and staff					
Provide professional development opportunities for faculty	Leadership Employees	Assist faculty in gaining skills and information needed to successfully obtain tenure	Libraries Faculty Personnel Officer provides peer-sharing sessions for faculty and staff to discuss Criterion B-D. Sessions allow new and existing faculty to learn from each other and gain strategies for success in these areas.	Retention of new hires	Offered as new faculty members are hired
				Satisfactory performance reviews	
			Libraries Faculty Personnel Officer provides orientation sessions for new librarians		
			Residency restructuring committee developed general orientation program for the incoming resident		
			New faculty have access to support through the mentoring program for tenure-track faculty		
Provide professional development opportunities for staff		Equip staff with tools for success within the libraries	Develop a supervisory skills training program for staff	Develop objectives for the training program	

Set to Print Landscape on Legal Paper

Create a healthy working environment for employees where differences are appreciated, respected, and valued

Goals	Diversity Category	Strategies	Tactics/Action	Assessment / Measurement	Timeline
Monitor diversity climate within the Libraries					
Be proactive in handling diversity and climate issues in order to create a healthy working environment	Leadership Employees	Conduct a diversity climate survey	Library wide diversity survey was conducted, results were reviewed and suggestions/recommendations discussed with Libraries administration	New initiatives resulting from survey results and recommendations	Diversity climate completed in 2006
		Collect/review informal feedback from employees on diversity and climate issues	Continue regular review of climate through formal/informal surveys and employee feedback.		Ongoing
			Conduct satisfaction survey to determine effectiveness of retention efforts		Survey on retention to be completed by spring 2010
	Students	Monitor library user surveys/comment cards for indications of service issues related to diversity			Ongoing

Goals	Diversity Category	Strategies	Tactics/Action	Assessment / Measurement	Timeline
Expand diversity training opportunities for the Libraries					
Create training programs and	Leadership	Create a working environment that	Provide informal educational opportunities	Favorable response from	Diversity video series

Set to Print Landscape on Legal Paper

10

Goals	Diversity Category	Strategies	Tactics/Action	Assessment / Measurement	Timeline
learning opportunities for faculty, staff, and administrators	Employees	promotes respect, understanding, and appreciation of differences	such as film series, book discussions, and exhibits on diversity related issues.	employees attending films and discussion	completed.
			In response to the diversity climate survey the Libraries held a year long diversity video series for employees highlighting a film every other month on a different aspect of diversity. Facilitators from U of L and the community lead discussions after the films.		
			Provide formal diversity training for libraries employees		Libraries plan to offer LGBT training in 2009

University Theme: Promote principles of diversity and social justice in educational opportunities, civic engagement and international awareness

▶ The Libraries encourage and promote diversity, social justice, global awareness, and civic engagement through educational exhibits and programs, outreach, and partnerships

Goals	Diversity Category	Strategies	Tactics/Action	Assessment / Measurement	Timeline
Increase extracurricular learning opportunities to broaden the horizons of our students so that they understand and value people of many cultural backgrounds					
Expand service learning and community internships	Leadership Training – students	Involve classes and individual students in service learning projects that allow them the opportunity to learn about different cultures while also helping others through giving and volunteerism	Libraries sponsored 2 events in 2007 and 2008 that included student curated exhibits and charity art auctions	Review participant evaluations to determine program success	
Devise and Implement a comprehensive plan for global awareness and engagement					
Develop a strong program for international visiting students	Leadership	Partner with community groups to provide work and educational experiences for visiting students.	The University Libraries participate in the Sister Cities Montpelier Work Exchange Program . Each year 1 or 2 college students from Montpelier France come to work for one month in the University Libraries. The experience	Completion of program	Ongoing summer program

Set to Print Landscape on Legal Paper

11

12

provides cross-cultural learning for the students and cultural immersion as they live, work and socialize in the community. A small salary and living stipend is provided to the students in the program.

Set to Print Landscape on Legal Paper

Goals	Diversity Category	Strategies	Tactics/Action	Assessment / Measurement	Timeline
Participate in mission-centered social and economic justice programs					
Promote recycling, energy conservation programs and other environmentally responsible practices	Leadership	Create a more sustainable environment Promote sustainability through provision of resources and programs for students and library users	Develop a plan to improve sustainability within the libraries, pending University planned energy audit Provide resources for students on sustainability issues Implement a recycling program Conduct a session for the Libraries on sustainable office practices	Completion of plan for the libraries	Resources available through Libraries website Recycling program developed in 2008 Session held 2008.
Develop excellence in bioethics and health care delivery disparities study and service	Leadership	Support research in the area of bioethics through library collections and programs	Kornhauser Library and Ekstrom Library are in the process of purchasing monographs in support of the new MA in Bioethics and Medical Humanities.	Continued growth of collection to support program	

Set to Print Landscape on Legal Paper

13

Goals	Diversity Category	Strategies	Tactics/Action	Assessment / Measurement	Timeline
Partner with organizations outside the Libraries to promote diversity					
Partner with other libraries and organizations to promote diversity	Leadership Employees	Create awareness of and advocacy around diversity issues within the profession	The Libraries were instrumental in efforts to bring the KLA/KSMA/SELA/ARL National Diversity in Libraries Conference to Louisville. The conference was held in October 2008	Program evaluations can be used to determine increase of awareness	Conference held in October 2008
			Librarians at U of L actively participated in planning and presented on diversity and library related topics with librarians from around the country		
Partner with other organizations on campus to promote diversity	Leadership Employees	Collaborate with University community to promote and further diversity efforts	Librarians serve in organizations and on committees such as CODRE, the Anne Braden Institute for Social Justice Research advisory board, and the University Diversity Chairs committee. Librarians also participate in UofL efforts such as the Strategic Partnership Initiative and Arts & Culture Partnership Initiative.	Increased library involvement in campus diversity efforts	Ongoing

Set to Print Landscape on Legal Paper

14

UMASS AMHERST LIBRARIES' COMMUNITY, DIVERSITY, AND SOCIAL JUSTICE ACTION PLAN

This action plan is written in response to the UMass Amherst Academic Affairs Community, Diversity, and Social Justice (CDSJ) Assessment Report issued in Fall 2003. In January 2002, the Academic Affairs CDSJ Team was constituted and charged with conducting an assessment as part of the campus-wide Community, Diversity, and Social Justice initiative. The Fall 2003 assessment report analyzes the results of the "Academic Affairs Survey of Employee Attitudes and Experiences" conducted in November 2002. In March 2004, Provost Charlena Seymour charged the Deans and Directors with developing action plans for their units on the basis of areas identified as calling for change. The key areas to be addressed in the action plans are Goals and Values, Personnel Policies, Work Environment, Management Practices, and Teaching and Learning.

In April 2004, Director of Libraries Jay Schafer tasked a Committee consisting of Allison Dolcey (Stacks Management Student Assistant), Michael Magrath (Stacks Management Supervisor), Anne C. Moore (Associate Director for User Services), Anne L. Moore (Access Services Coordinator), Kathy Nowicki (Serials and Microforms Assistant), and Dianna Williams (Assistant Director for Human Resources) to develop a CDSJ action plan for the UMass Amherst Libraries. Ninety library staff members replied to the November 2002 survey, a 70% response rate. The areas of concern identified in the library survey results include a lack of respect felt across job classifications (particularly by classified staff), outdated job descriptions, and lack of diversity within the Library staff. Therefore, the committee focused on writing actions that would address these areas of concern. The Committee drafted a plan outlining broad goals and specific actions which they believe will move the Library forward in creating a community committed to diversity and social justice. To ensure success, the Action Plan specifies the groups responsible for implementing each action and its intended start and completion date.

The CDSJ Action Plan draft was submitted to the Library's Senior Management Group and Staff Council for review and comment. Each of those groups solicited input regarding the draft from library staff. The CDSJ Action Plan was also a topic for discussion at an All Staff Meeting. This final plan was approved by the Senior Management Group on January 19, 2005 with the expectation that it will position the Library as a model of CDSJ activity on campus.

Definitions

Community: An interactive environment which values the richness and differences of individuals and cultures while affirming our common humanity.

Diversity: A range of human, social and cultural characteristics which shapes our sense of self and our relationship to the social world.

Social Justice: Efforts to eradicate exclusion and promote full and equal inclusion and participation for all social groups.

[From pages 4 & 5, The CDSJ Initiative: A New Approach to Community, Diversity and Social Justice. *http://www.umass.edu/ohr/cdsj_report1.htm*]

1 of 10

I. *Addressing Goals and Values*

A. **Enhance the sense of community in the Library.**

Action	Implementation	Start Date	Completion Date
1. Revise the Library's Mission Statement to reflect its commitment to community, diversity, and social justice.	Senior Management Group Staff Council	January 2005	May 2005
2. Provide opportunities for social interactions to build community—staff picnics, holiday party, "sherry" party or end-of-semester celebration, social time after all-staff meetings, etc.	Staff Council	Spring 2005	On-going
3. Involve more staff in the work of the Library during the semester; e.g., staffing extended hours before and during exams, staffing the Information Desk during the first two weeks of the semester, welcoming guests to events, assisting with the setup of displays. Provide necessary training.	User Services Division, but participation by all	Spring 2005	On-going
4. Create a Staff Development Committee to recommend and facilitate staff training and enrichment opportunities.	Director of Libraries	February 2005	On-going
5. Sponsor "What We Are Reading" program—select a book to read, post a list of what staff recommends to read, host minority author book signings and discussions, which are open to the public.	Staff Council	Spring 2005	On-going
6. Host brown-bag lunches once a month with a film or speaker.	Events Committee	Spring 2005	On-going

2 of 10

I. Addressing Goals and Values

B. Increase respect between classified and professional staff.

Action	Implementation	Start Date	Completion Date
1. Establish program of in-depth departmental orientations for both professional and classified staff. This may initially be targeted to new and transfer staff.	Staff Development Committee	January 2005	On-going
2. Present an open house each month wherein staff of one department address their on-going functions and new initiatives to library-wide audience in a social environment.	Events Committee	Spring 2005	On-going
3. Create teams of professional and classified staff to teach skills/make presentations to other staff; e.g., Web skills/GUI for using MilCirc, ExLibris.	Staff Development Committee	Spring 2005	On-going
4. Award matching funds from the Staff Development endowment to provide opportunities for staff to attend staff development programs.	Staff Development Committee	Spring 2005	On-going
5. Present brown-bag lunches for reports and updates about conferences and workshops attended as well as publications.	Senior Management Group Staff Development Committee	Spring 2005	On-going

3 of 10

I. Addressing Goals and Values

C. Enhance sense of community for Library staff within the campus.

Action	Implementation	Start Date	Completion Date
1. Assign liaisons to service departments on campus—Everywoman's Center, Stonewall Center, Disability Services, Alumni Affairs, Housing, Campus Activities Office, Athletics.	Associate Directors Liaison Council	January 2005	On-going
2. Create an Events Committee to coordinate Library events, including some open to the campus community.	Director of Libraries Staff Council	February 2005	On-going
3. Involve the Library in campus activities by opening the scheduling of Library meeting and event space to the campus.	Senior Management Group	Fall 2005	On-going

4 of 10

II. *Addressing Personnel Policies*

A. Increase the diversity of the professional and classified staff in the University Library. Recruit professional and classified staff from diverse backgrounds.

Action	Implementation	Start Date	Completion Date
1. Research additional sources for advertising vacant positions to target minority applicants.	Assistant Director for Human Resources CDSJ Team	January 2005	On-going
2. Support staff and student Library assistants who wish to attend library school with mentoring.	CDSJ Team	Spring 2005	On-going
3. Investigate adding descriptive information about the Library and the Amherst campus to our vacancy postings.	Assistant Director for Human Resources CDSJ Team	January 2005	On-going
4. Apply for a grant (possibly from the Institute of Museum and Library Services -IMLS) to establish a minority residency or internship program.	Director of Libraries Director of Library Development & Communications CDSJ Team	Spring 2005	Depends on Grant Application Process
5. Continue to offer workshops for staff on a broad spectrum of diversity topics.	CDSJ Team Staff Development Committee	Spring 2005	On-going
6. Investigate additional retention incentives; i.e., a mentoring program.	CDSJ Team	Spring 2005	On-going

5 of 10

III. *Addressing Management Practices*

A. Ensure all Library job descriptions are accurate and up to date.

Action	Implementation	Start Date	Completion Date
1. Develop and implement a new procedure for updating classified job descriptions, including All Staff Meeting with campus Human Resources personnel.	Assistant Director for Human Resources Senior Management Group	January 2005	March 2005
2. Revise all Form 30s within the Library	Assistant Director for Human Resources Senior Management Group	January 2005	December 2005
3. Revise all professional job descriptions	Assistant Director for Human Resources Senior Management Group	January 2005	August 2005
4. Encourage the University to work with the state to update Library job classifications in Massachusetts.	Director of Libraries Assistant Director for Human Resources	January 2005	On-going

6 of 10

IV. *Addressing Work Environment*

A. Improve the work environment, both in the Libraries and on campus, and position the Library as a model in diversity and social justice for the campus and community.

Action	Implementation	Start Date	Completion Date
1. For users and staff, create a prominent announcement space to promote campus wide activities and information, perhaps starting with something as simple as a bulletin board, and progressing to include an information presentation system. This should be included in the plans for a learning commons. Postings and information should be actively sought through contact with campus organizations.	Events Committee	Spring 2005	On-going
2. Post information about cultural, national, and religious holidays on the Intranet.	CDSJ Team	Spring 2005	On-going
3. Include student representatives on Staff Council and other Library committees.	Staff Council Student Supervisors	Spring 2005	On-going

4. Improve the working climate for our student workers by:
a. Hosting activities to show our appreciation of student employees with departmental and Library-wide pizza lunches.
b. Open some Staff Development training to students, particularly customer service- and diversity-related training.
c. Encourage student growth and retention by providing opportunities to change job assignments and to assume increasingly more complex work assignments.
	a. Events Committee
	   Student Supervisors
	b. Staff Development Committee
	   CDSJ Team
	c. Human Resources
	   Student Supervisors
		a. Spring 2005
		
		b. Spring 2005
		
		c. Spring 2005
			a. On-going
			
			b. On-going
			
			c. On-going

5. Provide a Library-wide student orientation each semester to build student knowledge and enhance performance.	Senior Management Group Student Supervisors	Spring 2005	On-going

7 of 10

V. Addressing Teaching and Learning

A. Create an atmosphere that is welcoming and comfortable as well as supportive to learning.

Action	Implementation	Start Date	Completion Date
1. Update furnishings	Administrative Services	Spring 2005	On-going
2. Improve lighting	Administrative Services	Spring 2005	On-going
3. Create a relaxed atmosphere by setting up more artwork and greenery.	Art & Exhibits Committee	Spring 2005	On-going
4. Improved signage	Senior Management Group Signage SWAT Team Administrative Services	Spring 2005	On-going
5. Create new or expand existing display areas through digitization and other means	Art & Exhibits Committee Special Collections & Archives	Spring 2005	On-going
6. Review and update exhibit procedures, so students and faculty can offer displays and artwork in the Library which reflect a diverse community.	Art & Exhibits Committee Senior Management Group	Spring 2005	On-going
7. Encourage faculty to display multicultural projects and hold events in the Library that they and their students have developed as part of their curricula	Liaison Council CDSJ Team Events Committee	Fall 2005	On-going
8. Create Web-based subject guides. Electronically distribute lists of new and relevant Library resources to faculty each semester. Ask faculty to discuss these resources with their students.	Liaison Council	Spring 2005	On-going

V. Addressing Teaching and Learning

A. Create an atmosphere that is welcoming and comfortable as well as supportive to learning. (Continued)

9. Strengthen tours and programs for international students and faculty by working with the International Programs Office.	User Services	Summer 2005	On-going
10. Create displays of books or art that highlight significant holidays or events from other cultures. Create reading lists to complement each display.	Art & Exhibits Committee	Fall 2005	On-going
11. Monitor access to Library services and facilities.	Health & Safety Committee Administrative Services	Spring 2005	On-going

V. Addressing Teaching and Learning

B. Insure access by all to the Library's resources and services.

Action	Implementation	Start Date	Completion Date
1. Expand the Archives and Special Collections online exhibit program.	Special Collections & Archives	Spring 2005	On-going
2. Invite members of the greater community to offer programs, workshops, art and displays that contribute to the education of the campus community concerning diversity and social justice.	CDSJ Team Events Committee Art & Exhibits Committee	Fall 2005	On-going
3. Partner with the Daily Collegian to write a series on the Library, including services offered, collection contents, and the history of the W.E.B. Du Bois Library.	Liaison Council Special Collections & Archives Director of Library Development & Communications	Spring 2005	On-going
4. Continue to distribute Library hours and information to Housing Services and RAs each fall for posting.	User Services	Spring 2005	On-going

V. Addressing Teaching and Learning

C. Enhance a sense of community for all Library users.

Action	Implementation	Start Date	Completion Date
1. Create a mural or display depicting places from which students, Library staff and student staff come, thus promoting a sense of identity and community.	CDSJ Team	Spring 2005	On-going
2. Create spaces specifically designed for students to congregate and talk.	Administrative Services	Spring 2005	On-going

V. Addressing Teaching and Learning

D. Enhance the awareness of social justice by Library users.

Action	Implementation	Start Date	Completion Date
1. Commission artwork to reflect the different ethnicities of the student population.	Art & Exhibits Committee Administrative Services	Fall 2005	On-going
2. Continue to publicize diversity programs and events taking place in either the community or on campus, with posters placed in areas where students gather.	CDSJ Team Art & Exhibits Committee	Spring 2005	On-going

University of Minnesota Libraries

Diversity Outreach Action Plan

Last Updated: August 19, 2009

From

Diversity Outreach Collaborative

2

Diversity Action Plan Draft 06/11/08 JLG

Purpose

The purposes of this Diversity Action Plan is:
- to provide background information about diversity efforts at the University of Minnesota related to the institution's strategic planning,
- to inform readers the University Libraries' (UL) steps towards a programmatic diversity initiative, and
- to list specific actions which initiate the official diversity program for the UL.

Background and Working Definition of Diversity

Diversity throughout the University of Minnesota system is an important theme in the University's commitment to transform itself into one of the top three research institutes in the world. The strategic positioning process included a System Wide Academic Task Force on Diversity. Beyond that, the issue of diversity arose in almost every task force report related to the U's strategic positioning. A diverse institutional community will contribute to faculty, staff and student retention through the creation of an inclusive supportive academic environment, and will lead to a level of academic excellence that supports the University's "top three" goal.

The System Wide Academic Task Force on Diversity states, "Diversity should be defined as the full range of human difference that influences access, equity, and relationships in living, learning, and working environments. These differences have resulted historically in under-representation and marginalization based on race, ethnicity, gender identity/expression, sexual orientation, religion, disability, age, socioeconomic status, geography, and citizenship status. In other words, the University will be truly diverse when differences among individuals are leveraged to strengthen and enrich learning, working, and social environments, instead of being viewed as a negative condition."

Background: Diversity Initiatives at the University of Minnesota

The full report of the System Wide Academic Task Force on Diversity (2004) is available at the following url: http://www1.umn.edu/systemwide/strategic_positioning/tf_sys_acad_diversity.html

Given the recommendations of the task force, the Office for Multicultural and Academic Affairs was reorganized and renamed the Office for Equity and Diversity (OED). Along with this new office at the University of Minnesota came the development of a new position, the Vice President and Vice Provost of Equity and Diversity. For the first time, the offices that work in the areas of diversity outreach had a position at the level of Vice President, filled in 2006 by Dr. Rusty Barceló.

> "Diversity is everybody's responsibility, from the president, provost, vice presidents, and on down to the very last person on the org chart. We all play a role."
>
> Dr. Rusty Barceló
>
> (Found at http://www1.umn.edu/umnnews/Feature_Stories/A_community_builder_for_diversity.html)

The OED spent its first year doing an environmental scan. Dr. Barceló met with community members across the state of Minnesota and students, faculty and staff at the University of Minnesota. The goal, vision and mission of the OED developed from these conversations and the work of the System-wide Task Force on Diversity.

University of Minnesota Libraries

A strong demonstration of the UL's commitment to diversity is the creation of the position of Outreach Librarian to Under Represented Groups in Academic Programs, aka the Diversity Outreach Librarian (DOL). The DOL works in partnership with faculty and other campus professionals to develop programs that extend library collections and services to traditionally underserved populations, with an emphasis on multicultural programs and students of color. This position is split 50/50 between the Multicultural Center for Academic Excellence, which reports to the OED, and the UL. The intent of

3

this split was to allow the person doing diversity outreach in the libraries to have a better understanding of how the offices that directly serves the multicultural undergraduate student population on campus work. Because diversity touches all people, no one person alone can work with all of the diversity populations. The DOL position should be seen as a supplemental position to the work that others have been doing for years both informally and formally.

The UL and DOL also partner with the Office of International Programs (OIP), because broad concerns about diversity include recognition and consideration of the needs of international students and scholars. The UL, OED, and OIP all serve large constituencies that cross departments, schools, units, programs, etc. As a result future programming must reflect a change in the institution's commitment. It is unlikely that isolated events and projects will impart the overall ideology that must take place for success in diversity.

It is worth mentioning that both the University of Minnesota Libraries and the Office for Equity and Diversity both serve large constituencies that cross departments, schools, units, programs, etc. It is unlikely that isolated events and projects will impart the overall ideology that must take place for success in diversity. During the past two years, the DOL conducted interviews and had both formal and informal discussions with staff from the OED, OIP, and the UL's Directors of Academic Programs. In all conversations it has been striking how mutually important the collaborations between the UL, OED and OIP are, yet none know exactly what a more formalized collaboration would look like. The DOL position and the Diversity Outreach Collaborative (see Appendix A) are to lead the charge in these matters. They will collaborate and provide best practices and resources for all staff within the libraries to utilize in their departmental planning, priority setting, and resource allocation regarding diversity issues and activities. In an effort to move forward with the development of both the DOL position and the Diversity Outreach Collaborative, this document (1) identifies and defines the current structures and collaborations between OED and UL and OIP and UL, and (2) presents the next steps for the UL to support diversity initiatives at the University of Minnesota.

Current University Libraries' Progress

Current collaborations between the UL and OED include the launch of the Bridge to Academic Excellence a six-week summer bridge program for incoming freshman from diverse backgrounds. The UL successfully integrated information literacy instruction into this program, and they continue to work on the development of this bridge program for summer 2008. This is a wonderful example of the types of collaborations in which the UL should participate; it is also an opportunity to create a toolkit or process to share with other bridge programs that request our assistance.

Another area that has been strongly impacted in the past two years is the outreach to the faculty and staff working with the multicultural student body. Information Literacy training and discussions have been ongoing in an effort to create strong allies within the ranks of those shown to be the first point of communication with undergraduates. Just as we aim to provide scholarly communication dialogues and research support to faculty in our departments, we should be providing those same liaison type services to the staff within the OED. Not only does the OED office and its affiliate units (see Appendix B) touch students, but its arm also reaches to the faculty and staff around campus.

Like any major program that is developed by the UL, diversity outreach will not be successful if designed in a silo. It is something that touches everyone and therefore everyone should have an opportunity to gain more knowledge and support in these areas. Just as we have expert help in the areas of departmental studies across campus, relevant expertise exists within the University of Minnesota to support diversity outreach efforts at the UL. Both the Diversity Outreach Collaborative and the DOL will make it a goal to provide a stable programmatic approach to working with diverse communities and create support (online and in person) for diversity issues across campus and the global society.

4

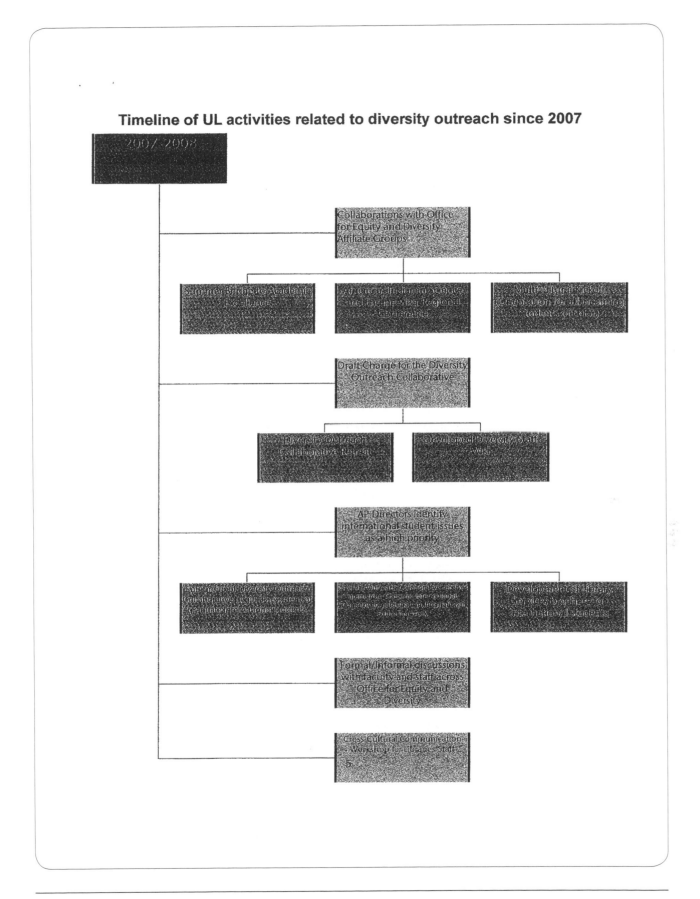

Timeline of UL activities related to diversity outreach since 2007

Diversity Action Plan Next Steps

In order for the libraries to move forward we will need to take the time to really commit to supporting diversity programming across all units. It is imperative that our diversity initiatives are supported in the UL's planning documents and goals. To begin developing an official diversity program at the UL, the following questions should be considered:

1. To what extent do the planning and design of our programs/projects/collections take into account the diversity that is currently in place and/or lacking at the University of Minnesota?

2. How do we create and review our programs/projects/collections to promote equity and success for all members of the University of Minnesota community?

It will be the role of the DOL and Collaborative to identify and collaborate with already existing programs within the UL and the University of Minnesota community to facilitate the conversations surrounding these questions.

GOAL: Create an official library outreach diversity program for the University of Minnesota Libraries

Strategy	Actions	Assigned to	Stakeholders	Target Implementation Date
Identify current public services and collections that promote diversity at the UL	• Create a list of events, collections and web pages • Develop promotional materials to enhance diversity awareness and to communicate projects and offerings at the UL	Diversity Outreach Collaborative	AP Departments, OED, Communications	September 2009 Ongoing Every other year
User needs assessments on diverse populations (ethnic, racial, international, sexual orientation and disability services)	• Do a literature review • Determine which evaluation tool to use • Disperse the assessment • Report results	Diversity Outreach Collaborative	AP Departments, IADS, OED, Communications	December 2009 Ongoing Every other year
Report status of goals and objectives from the Diversity Outreach Collaborative on a quarterly basis	• Issue reports and updates to the AP Directors and Libraries Leadership Cabinet including information on activities and training	Diversity Outreach Collaborative	AP Directors, Libraries Leadership Cabinet, OED, Communications	July 2009 Ongoing Quarterly See appendix D.
Provide diverse programming that promotes the understanding and celebration of differences as well as similarities	• Encourage celebrations, storytelling, and cross-cultural learning via staff events, speakers, as well as	All Units		Ongoing

6

	informal methods			
Support and advocate for the inclusion of diversity-driven educational initiatives across campus	• Develop a way to formally submit diversity programming initiatives through the Diversity Outreach Collaborative • Develop a formal set of guidelines and program tools for library units to use in their work with diverse programs	Diversity Outreach Collaborative	All Units	Summer 2009
Identify a small number of high impact or signature programs that the Libraries should initiate in the coming year.	• Review current efforts at high impact programs	Diversity Outreach Collaborative	AP, OED, Communications	Ongoing
Develop a curriculum/outline/plan for cultural competency training for staff at the Libraries to support service to external communities	Staff Education and Development Diversity Outreach Librarian Diversity Outreach Collaborative	Diversity Outreach Collaborative	Public Service units of UL OED SED	Fall 2009

7

UNL Libraries Diversity Plan 2010-11

Best Practices to Recruit and Retain a Diverse Faculty

Goals

- Create a positive work environment that empowers the creativity and diversity of all individuals
- Increase the recruitment of individuals from underrepresented groups in faculty and staff positions.
- Develop ways to assess diversity efforts
- Encourage and reward diversity and multicultural initiatives within the organizational structure.

In less than a decade, the UNL Libraries, through recruitment and retention efforts, have increased the number of minority librarians from 2.6% of the faculty in 1999 to 12% in 2008.

Fig. 1 UNL Libraries Faculty Statistics 1999-2009.

Year	Libraries Total Faculty	Libraries Minority Faculty	% of Total Faculty
1999-00	38	1	2.6%
2000-01	39	2	5.1%
2001-02	42	2	4.8%
2002-03	40	2	5.0%
2003-04	39	2	5.1%
2004-05	44	2	4.5%
2005-06	49	3	6.1%
2006-07	49	3	6.1%
2007-08	49	4	8.2%
2008-09	49	6	12.2%

Scout

Develop relationships with racial and ethnic organizations to increase accessibility to potential candidates
- Participate in ARL diversity initiatives, Initiative to Recruit a Diverse Workforce and Leadership and Career Development Program (LCDP). Library administrators (Dean Giesecke and others) continue to present seminars and serve as mentors to minority librarians.
- Support active membership and participation in the racial and ethnic organization and other diversity related committees i.e. disabilities, LGBTQA
- Participate and attend conferences such as the ARL National Diversity in Libraries conference and the Joint Conference for Librarians of Color.

1

UNL Libraries Diversity Plan 2010-11

Best Practices to Recruit and Retain a Diverse Faculty

Develop relationships with undergraduate students and provide informal mentoring about careers in the library profession

- Develop a student worker interest group similar to a "grow your own program". This group will allow librarians to build relationships to informally mentoring student workers and introduce them to careers in library and information science.
- Create Center for Digital Research in the Humanities (CDRH) internships with underrepresented groups in library schools
- Participate in Institute for Ethnic Studies celebration events with UNL faculty and students to discuss career opportunities in library and information sciences.

Participate in local regional and national career fairs

- Increase awareness of opportunities at the University of Nebraska-Lincoln by sending fellowship and scholarship opportunities to UNL Career Services
- Develop awareness of opportunities in library profession by participating in UNL Alumni of Color Career Forum, Career Services

Search

Improve the diversity of search candidate pools by utilizing active recruitment methods to solicit applications of diverse individuals who may not have considered moving to Nebraska.

- Send job announcements to targeted prospective applicant groups, i.e. Spectrum scholars, Knowledge River, ARL Leadership and Career Development Program, ACRL Residency Interest Group
- Attend conferences and personally invite individuals to apply for a particular position. This type of hands-on recruitment provides a friendly face to applicants who may have never considered Nebraska as a possible employment opportunity.
- Review job posting information for faculty & staff positions.
  - o Expand efforts in advertising faculty job announcements in multicultural social networks, blogs, listserv, and email.
  - o Examine efforts to recruit underrepresented staff in the region.
  - o Work with UNL Equity Access and Diversity to obtain statistics about the diversity of the search pools

Augment Library Search Committee Training

- Review research on implicit bias and share info with committee
  Discuss views on diversity and other controversial topics
- Review information in Search committee policies and procedures
  - o include new information about Assumptions and Biases, Work Life Balance UNL flyer, About Lincoln Diversity (Ethnic Studies information)identifies ethnic services and businesses in Lincoln
  - o Review best practices to recruit candidates to Lincoln to live and work

Support

2

UNL Libraries Diversity Plan 2010-11

Best Practices to Recruit and Retain a Diverse Faculty

Support for non-tenured Junior Faculty of Color to attain tenure and promotion.
- Provide mentoring opportunities with tenured faculty
- Provide financial support for professional development opportunities.
- Provide research and grant writing support

Support the collaborative efforts of a Multicultural Services Team to assist in the recruit and retain of faculty of color.
- Support and encourage collaborative efforts for research, publishing, and grant writing

Collaborate with Library Faculty to develop professional development track information for all faculty.
- Early career opportunities: Minnesota Institute for Early Career Librarians from Traditionally Underrepresented Groups, ALA Emerging Leaders Program
- Midcareer opportunities: ACRL Immersion, ARL Leadership and Career Development Program, Nebraska Library Leadership Institute, Mountain Plains Library Association Leadership Institute
- Leadership opportunities: Harvard Leadership Institute for Academic Librarians (ACRL), Senior Fellows Program UCLA Scholars, Spectrum Doctoral Fellowship

Sustain

Provide financial support for professional development opportunities.
- Identify fellowships and scholarships available to offset financial requirements

Collaborate with Faculty to identify professional recognition awards, fellowships and honors to recognize outstanding service.
- Encourage nominations of these individuals to receive such accolades, i.e. ALA Movers and Shakers, Zora Neale Hurston Award

Encourage leadership experiences in library and state organization and within the university.
- Nebraska Library Association, ACRL, UNL Faculty Senate

Continue to develop and assess inclusive work climate issues.
- Utilize the information from the ClimateQUAL survey to develop diversity education programs
- Incorporate cultural competencies into the NU Values & faculty evaluations
  - Work with the library administration and staff development officer to identify appropriate components
- Evaluate the role of the Diversity Committee within library organization.
  - Expand the role in decision, policy making, and strategic planning in the library

3

UNL Libraries Diversity Plan 2010-11

Best Practices to Recruit and Retain a Diverse Faculty

- o Collaborate with the Assessment Committee in developing methods to assess diversity initiatives and climate issues
- o Increase library-wide participation to diversity programs and activities which can be linked to cultural competencies
- o Acknowledge and reward efforts for diversity/multicultural efforts in the library

4

Rutgers University Libraries

Diversity Plan

2009-2010

The Rutgers University Libraries formed a Diversity Advisory Committee in 1995. This committee is charged with providing advice on issues of diversity. The overall goal of the library diversity program is to assure that all library personnel and library users feel welcomed, valued, and respected and to assure that library personnel, services, and collections appropriately reflect the diversity of the Rutgers community and its curriculum and research interests. In addition our overarching goal is to ensure that diversity is an integral part of the organizational culture of the Libraries. To accomplish this, the Committee provides advice to the University Librarian on programs or policies affecting staff development, recruitment, retention, public services, and collections.

In addition to the activities of the Diversity Advisory Committee the Libraries have engaged in a comprehensive diversity education effort known as *Blueprint for Diversity* which is focused on library personnel but is open to all interested members of the University community.

Further, the Libraries are also committed to recruiting a more diverse workforce to support the needs of our diverse user community.

Definition: The concept of diversity encompasses acceptance and respect. It means understanding that each individual is unique, and recognizing our individual differences. These can be along the dimensions of race, ethnicity, gender, sexual orientation, socio-economic status, age, physical abilities, religious beliefs, or other ideologies. It is the exploration of these differences in a safe , positive, and nurturing environment. It is about understanding each other and moving beyond simple tolerance to embracing and celebrating the rich dimensions of diversity contained within each individual.

(http://gladstone.uoregon.edu/~asuomca/diversityinit/definition.html)

The following plan connects all these efforts to deepen and enrich the experiences and awareness of diversity at the Libraries.

Rutgers University Libraries' Diversity Plan provides the basis to foster and support a culture of diversity within the libraries' workforce, its collections, and services to users. To expedite this plan, the University Librarian and Vice President for Information Services, the Director for Administrative Services as diversity officer for the Libraries, and the Diversity Advisory Committee along with all faculty and staff commit themselves to achieving the following goals within the stated time frames:

1.   Diversity Recruitment

    Goal: To significantly increase diversity among Library faculty and staff

Implementation: Libraries Human Resources, Search Committees

Within 6 months: Review recruitment procedures to clarify Libraries' commitment to diversity.

> Complete review of intern/residency program to ensure its effectiveness as well as complete revised program

> Utilize hiring opportunities as appropriate especially Target of Opportunity and Cluster Hiring.

Within 12 months:

> Establish mentoring program or discussion/support group for staff members who want to pursue a library degree

> Develop a program for promoting the Libraries as a career destination for students by establishing mentored work opportunities

> Utilize hiring opportunities as appropriate including Target of Opportunity and Cluster Hiring.

2. Diversity Retention

   Goal: Continue diversity education and programs of the Diversity Committee as a way of creating a supportive environment for a diverse staff.

   Implementation: Library Human Resources, Diversity Committee and Staff Development

   Within 12 months:

   > Expand mentoring and orientation programs for new staff

   > Enhance management development opportunities for supervisors and managers

   > Offer skills training for staff

3. Diversity and Organizational Culture

   Goal: Instill the importance of diversity in all staff members at all levels so that diversity is inherent in the culture of the Libraries

   Implementation: Libraries Human Resources, Staff Development, Cabinet, Diversity Committee

   Within 12 months:

Offer at least 3 programs that are both instructive and engaging on diversity related issues.

Review diversity opportunities related to their areas of responsibility with each Cabinet member quarterly. Opportunities should include recruitment, retention and information and technical aspects of library services.

Goal: Create a multicultural resources website/portal (subject resources) for libraries as well as external audiences.

Implementation: Diversity committee members, librarians

Within 12 months:

Present Web pages content that will be linked via the Libraries Diversity Resources page as well as Research Resources pages.

The Committee recommends that this Diversity plan and its goals should be reviewed by Cabinet twelve months from the date of its issuance. Further, all the goals listed herein should be considered as part of the Libraries Strategic Plan and should be cross-referenced in that document.

A Research Library for a Major University

The Strategic Plan for the
University Libraries of Virginia Tech
Operating Plan 2003~04

Tasks for the year are in bold black. Note that all objectives are not necessarily tasked for this year.

Mission

The University Libraries at Virginia Tech provide and promote access to information resources for the achievement of the University's objectives in teaching, learning, research, creativity, and community service.

We are dedicated to meeting the information, curricular and research needs of students, faculty, and staff of the Virginia Tech community, wherever located, in a manner that respects the diversity of community and ideas.

We provide selected services to a wider community of users.

Values

We are defined by our core commitment to the sharing of what humanity has discovered and thought. We value:

- *Information*, whose free flow throughout the university provides an accurate basis for its work

- *Ideas*, the university's defining occupation

- *Knowledge*, which preserves the progress of past generations

- *Discovery*, which builds the future

- *Truth,* which guides our interactions with one another and with our public

Vision

We will be collaborative partners with members of the university community as we collectively work to position the university as a top-tier research institution. Wherever they are located, members of the Virginia Tech community will be supported by the library as they engage in research, as they share in quality learning experiences at the undergraduate and graduate levels, and as they work in transferring knowledge and expertise between the university and society.

Goal 7
Staff
We will employ sufficient numbers of knowledgeable, adaptable, and user-directed faculty and staff.

Hire additional faculty and staff needed to provide the excellent library resources and services essential to a top-tier research university
Establish the Library Diversity Committee
New in 2003-04

Participate in ASERL/SOLINET conference "Diversity in Libraries" May 2004.
New in 2003-04

Establish and fill Outreach librarian position in the Instruction/Reference unit
New in 2003-04

Establish new learning opportunities for library faculty and staff relevant to personal professional growth in the context of library objectives and operations
Plan, implement and assess a program of training that will support data-driven decision making.
Continues in 2003-04

Plan, implement and assess an orientation program for new employees.
Continues in 2003-04

Identify ways in which the new program of training paths might link to the University's mandatory job dimensions (diversity, safety, teamwork) for classified staff.
Continues in 2003-04

Recognize and reward performance of library faculty and staff commensurate with a major research institution
Implement the library recognition program.
New in 2003-04

1/8/2004   *9*

UW Libraries Diversity Plan 2005

The Libraries Diversity and Organizational Culture Task Force was charged in March of 2004 to develop a diversity plan. The Task Force reviewed relevant UW documents and also looked at plans and practices in other universities. In 2004 the Task Force surveyed library staff in order to identify issues of diversity important to the staff and identify areas that need attention or improvement. Survey results showed diversity is important to our staff, and that the most important issue is being able to support our diverse user community effectively (Appendix 1). However, the staff also perceives that the Libraries can do a better job in addressing diversity issues, especially in recruiting a diverse work force and in supporting the needs of our diverse user community.

At the same time the Libraries' Diversity Task Force was working on the survey and plan, the University of Washington was conducting a Diversity Appraisal. The Appraisal Steering Committee asked all units across all three campuses to document their diversity initiatives and practices. The Diversity Appraisal is just one of many ways the UW administration is seeking to incorporate greater awareness of diversity issues into University operations. It is within this culture of diversity awareness that the Libraries' Task Force has written this plan.

The University of Washington defines diversity broadly to include "race, gender, disability, class, sexual identity/orientation, religion, age, ethnicity, culture, region/geography, and indigenous status."

Respect for all human diversity is a fundamental value of the Libraries and is identified among the core values of our strategic plan. Staff members who appreciate different backgrounds and perspectives provide us with a competitive advantage as we approach problem solving and planning for services. This appreciation also allows us to serve our increasingly diverse communities more effectively and with more sensitivity.

Beyond respect for diversity, it is important to recognize that inequity can often accompany diversity. This plan is meant to foster and support an organizational culture where those inequities do not occur or are remedied when identified.

Libraries personnel at all levels of the organization are responsible for developing and maintaining a culture supportive of and committed to diversity. However, in order to expedite implementation of the plan and provide support and guidance, the Diversity Task Force recommends that the establishment of a Diversity Officer position and a standing Diversity Committee be the first actions taken (see Goal #5). The Diversity Officer and Committee should begin action on the "within 6 months" items immediately as they are of the highest priority. The remaining action items where implementation is recommended within twelve months should be prioritized by the Committee. Where funds and workload implications of others are incurred in the execution of the Plan, the responsible party(ies) will develop a plan.

1. Recruitment of staff from diverse backgrounds
   Goal: To increase the diversity of the Libraries' workforce at all levels of the organization

   Action Items:

   Implementation: Diversity Officer; Diversity Committee; Administrative Officer Responsible for Personnel (AORP); Staff Development

   Within 6 Months

- Review our recruitment policies and procedures so that they support the UW Libraries commitment to diversity
- Initiate a conversation between the iSchool Diversity Committee and the Libraries Diversity Committee to explore collaboration
- Investigate the costs and effectiveness of residency programs for minority librarians and develop a proposal if appropriate (2005-2006)

Within 12 Months
- Establish mentoring program for staff who may want to pursue a library degree, collaborating with the i-School
- Work with the University to take advantage of hiring opportunities that promote a diverse Libraries staff
- Proactively promote UW Libraries as a place in which to work
- Establish opportunities for students interested in working in libraries as a career to participate in mentored work programs

2. Retention of staff from diverse backgrounds
Goal: Promote an inclusive and supportive workplace culture as an important element in retaining a diverse staff

Action Items:

Within 12 Months
- Support opportunities for professional development and/or growth, and mentoring/networking for all staff
Implementation: Diversity Officer; Diversity Committee; Libraries Council; Staff Development; Librarian Advisory Program (LAP)
- Facilitate connections between new hires and groups/resources at the university and in the community
Implementation: Diversity Committee; Diversity Officer; Staff Development Officer, UL Staff
- Work with the University to enhance salary and compensation flexibility to retain a diverse library staff
Implementation: Dean of the Libraries; AORP

3. Organizational Culture
Goal: To incorporate awareness of the value and importance of diversity at all levels of the Libraries so that staff recognize their responsibility in maintaining a culture supportive of and committed to diversity; provide a supportive and safe working and learning environment

Action Items:

Implementation: Diversity Officer; Diversity Committee; Staff Development

Within 6 months
- Provide ongoing staff training to foster individual responsibility for maintenance of a supportive and safe working and learning environment, with particular attention to the role of supervisors and managers to eliminate or remedy inequities when they are identified
- Highlight and promote the diversity of the libraries staff through programs and publications throughout the organization, i.e. Inforum, Library Directions, and LSA
- Enhance the Staff Development collection with diversity related materials including academic librarianship, higher education and organizational development

4. Services to Constituents

Goal: To enrich the quality of life and advance intellectual discovery by connecting people of diverse backgrounds and ethnicities with knowledge

Action Items:

Within 6 Months
- Develop and implement ongoing staff training in order to improve staff members' abilities to provide excellent service to all our diverse users, especially with regards to primary language barriers and physical/mental disabilities.
  Implementation: Staff Development Officer; Diversity Committee; RISG and other public service groups
- To ensure compliance with Section 508 of the Americans with Disabilities Act, attempt to procure accessible information technology products and electronic resources. If an accessible product cannot be found, ask vendors about their plans for making future versions of their products accessible and let them know that accessibility is a consideration for purchase.
  Implementation: CMS; Diversity Officer
- Review University of Washington Libraries' publications, website, and service policies for their accessibility to disabled users.
  Implementation: WSC; RISG, Publications Committee

Within 12 Months
- Develop and maintain collections to support diversity in the current and changing UW curriculum
  Implementation: IRC; Liaisons; Cataloging Policy Committee; Metadata Implementation Group
- Increase outreach to UW and external communities through library resources, services, collections, web resources and exhibits related to diversity; including the use of multilingual web pages and other publications as appropriate.
  Implementation: WSC; Liaisons; IRC
- Provide services and spaces that nurture and support academic success for our diverse student community

5. Organizational Structure of Diversity in the Libraries
   Goal: To create a standing Diversity Committee, reporting directly to the Dean of University Libraries

   Membership:
   - Half of the committee membership should come from the Task Force to ensure continuity
   - The Staff Development Officer and the Assessment Officer will serve as ex officio members of the Committee to aid in communication, implementation, and benchmarking.
   - Consider the inclusion of 1 member from outside the Libraries

   Elements to consider for inclusion in the charge to the Diversity Committee:
   - Coordinate implementation of the diversity plan
   - Promote the inclusion of diversity into our culture/organizational values
   - Review and assess the diversity plan and staff/community needs annually, including the establishment of appropriate benchmarks to measure and ensure progress in achieving the goals and action items
   - Work with other library individuals and groups to identify and take advantage of opportunities related to diversity
   - Provide a "diversity toolkit" for Libraries staff to use in outreach
   - Establish and maintain a website and use other appropriate methods of communicating with staff and community about diversity

Goal: To establish the position of the Diversity Officer

Responsibilities of the Diversity Officer, based on an initial 2 year half-time appointment include:

- Chair the Diversity Committee
- Provide oversight for the Libraries' diversity efforts
- Serve as official liaison to UW offices and departments, i.e. Office of Minority Affairs on behalf of the UW Libraries and the Diversity Committee
- Work with the Diversity Committee and others in identifying areas of needed support within the Libraries, i.e. training
- Assist in identifying opportunities for libraries staff involvement in diversity activities on campus and outreach to the community
- Be involved in professional association diversity programs/committees
- Assist individuals, management and library units in achieving goals of the diversity plan and other diversity initiatives
- Serve ex-officio on Libraries Council

It is the recommendation of the Task Force that a review of the Diversity Officer be conducted after 2 years. This review, involving Libraries Cabinet and the Diversity Committee, should include consideration of the placement of the position in the organization as well as the time commitment of the position.

**Yale University Library
Strategic Plan for Diversity and Inclusion
2009-2011**

**Prepared by the
Yale University Library
Diversity Council**

**Revised from 2006 original,
June 2009**

Mary Caldera
Chair

Yale University Library   1   Diversity Strategic Plan

Table of Contents:

Yale University Library
Diversity and Inclusion Strategic Plan
2009-2011

Purpose and Vision

In 2004, employees of the Yale University Library (YUL) participated in the Yale University Workplace Survey Pilot. In response to the results of the survey, the Library Management Council (LMC) identified diversity as a focus area for the library.

Therefore, the Yale University Library Diversity Council was formed in August 2005 to enhance the diversity and cultural competence of our staff so that our workplace continues to evolve into an even more inclusive and congenial environment. This type of atmosphere is conducive to job satisfaction and will in turn lead to even more effective service to our diverse patrons.

The Diversity Council is taking a leading role in developing and implementing initiatives that promote diversity and inclusion within our staff community. Diversity includes, but is not limited to, visible and invisible attributes such as age, gender, gender identity, physical ability, sexual orientation, religion, race, national origin, cultural heritage, and ethnic background. Recognizing diversity is a key component of excellence in the workplace that allows individuals to reach their full potential. The Diversity Council strives to provide a positive work environment which is free of any form of bigotry, harassment, intimidation, threat, or abuse, whether verbal or written, physical or psychological, direct or implied.

The Diversity Council views multiculturalism and pluralism as essential components of its mission and work. The Diversity Council will work in conjunction and in partnership with YUL and Yale University's Office of Diversity to attain this vision. Valuing diversity and practicing inclusion is in the YUL's core values, and in our interpersonal working relationships at all levels. YUL will achieve and sustain diversity and inclusion for our employees, clientele, and educational partners.

Charge

The Yale University Library Diversity Council was formed to enhance the diversity and cultural competence of our staff so that our workplace continues to evolve into an even more open and congenial environment. This type of atmosphere is conducive to job satisfaction and will in turn lead to even more effective service to our diverse patrons. The sponsor of the Diversity Council is the University Librarian.

Goals, Strategies and Success Measures

The Workplace Survey provided the Diversity Council with YUL-specific data on diversity issues that require immediate attention. While the Diversity Council defines diversity to include many varied attributes, it focused its initial efforts on goals relating to race and ethnicity and have expanded to include other areas of diversity including class. The following three goals were generated by the Diversity Council as the initial priorities for enhancing diversity at YUL and continue to be our top priorities. As YUL and the Diversity Council achieve each of these goals, new and additional goals will be generated by the Diversity Council to meet the changing needs for the continued improvement in YUL's diverse workplace.

Goal #1: Recruitment and Retention.

By 2011 Yale University Library will achieve a significant increase in the hiring and promotion of diverse staff in vacancies in both Clerical and Technical (especially at D and E levels) and Management and Professional positions.

Strategy #1: Library Human Resources and the Diversity Council will work with department heads to proactively identify and implement strategies to recruit diverse internal candidates for positions within their departments. These strategies include, but are not limited to, phone calls to colleagues, networking, and brainstorming with department staff on ways to increase diversity.

Strategy #2: Library Human Resources and the Diversity Council will work to document best practices on recruitment and retention of a diverse workforce at all levels for use by hiring supervisors.

Strategy 4#: Each year YUL and the Diversity Council will host a day-long gathering of scholars from the ARL initiative to Recruit a Diverse Workforce, and/or other similar groups, with meetings, tours, presentations, and other activities.

Measurement #1: A marked increase in the diversity of the applicant pool for upper level C/T positions and M/P ranks.

Measurement #2: Annual increase in the number of members of underrepresented groups hired and retained for both C/T top level and M/P mid-level positions.

Goal #2: Climate and Culture.

By 2011, Yale University Library will demonstrate a measurable improvement in the climate and culture of diversity and inclusion.

Strategy #1: In an effort to heighten awareness of diversity in the Library, the Diversity Council will work with Library Human Resources, the Library Staff Association (LiSA), and the Standing Committee on Professional Awareness (SCOPA) to organize staff training on diversity.

[Mandatory diversity training for all staff was completed in June 2008. Training for new staff TBD by the University-wide diversity training schedule.]

Strategy #2: YUL and the Diversity Council will collaborate to coordinate diversity-related lectures given by Yale community members and/or outside speakers and publicize relevant web based resources.

Strategy #3: The Diversity Council will work with Library Human Resources to refine performance appraisals, especially those of supervisors, to include job behaviors that contribute to recruiting and retaining a diverse staff.

Strategy #4: The Diversity Council will participate in the second university-wide workplace survey and check for data indicating improved perceptions of the library climate.

Measurement #1: By the end of the 2011 calendar year, all YUL supervisors will have attended at least one diversity training session. [Measure accomplished in June 2008. Training for new staff TBD by the University-wide diversity training schedule.]

Measurement #2: There will be diversity-related lectures at least once each term (fall, spring, summer).

Measurement #3: There will be a measurable improvement of scores on diversity-related questions in the Yale University Workplace Survey 2010.

Goal #3: Career Growth and Internal Mobility

By 2010, Yale University Library will have increased the number of internal candidates from underrepresented groups for job vacancies.

Strategy #1: YUL will publicize opportunities for Library staff to participate in career advancement, training, and cross-training programs in order to provide equal opportunities for learning, advancement and promotion within the Library

Strategy #2: The Diversity Council will work with Library Human Resources to develop supervisor competencies by developing programs, such as those that teach coaching and mentoring skills, which will encourage the promotion and advancement of C/T and M/P employees.

Strategy #3: The Diversity Council will work with Library Human Resources to create internships for library staff and MLS diverse students.

Strategy #6: The Diversity Council will work with Library Human Resources to actively support Library staff who wish to obtain a Master of Library Science, Information Studies, or other library-related degree, and utilize employees' library knowledge and experience for career advancement.

Yale University Library   5   Diversity Strategic Plan

Measurement #1: By 2011, a significant number of C/T vacancies at higher levels have been filled by internal candidates from underrepresented groups.

Measurement #2: Statistics will show that an employee's time within a certain grade has no more than a 20% range from least time-in-grade to most time-in-grade across for every library employee.

Measure #3: Staff indicate that they are treated fairly, have the same opportunity to succeed as peers as measured by a significant improvement in Yale Workplace Survey results.

Yale University Library   6   Diversity Strategic Plan

Diversity Group Charge

Home   Services   Get Help   About Us

search library site   [Search]

UNIVERSITY LIBRARY
UNIVERSITY OF ILLINOIS AT URBANA-CHAMPAIGN

Ask A Librarian   Contact Us   My Library Account

Library Committee Handbook
-- Index of Committees
-- Planning Calendar

Diversity Committee

Committee Charge

Agendas and Minutes

Diversity Goals 2007-2012

Diversity and Multicultural Information

_____

E-mail:
diversity@library.uiuc.edu

Library » Committees » Library Diversity Committee » Charge and Membership

Library Diversity Committee Charge and Membership

Charge

The Library Diversity Committee provides leadership and guidance to the Library by encouraging awareness about and discussions of diversity. Specifically, the Committee will focus on diversity issues with regard to Library climate, staff training and development, services to patrons, and campus outreach.

Working with the Outreach Librarian for Multicultural Services, the Staff development and Training Advisory Committee, and the Human Resources Office, the Library Diversity Committee will establish and prioritize goals regarding the provision of diversity services and training. The Committee will also plan and promote diversity activities within the Library. Finally, the Committee will support, if and when appropriate, the work of the Library's Affirmative action Officer and Equal Employment Opportunity Committee.

Composition

The Committee is appointed by the University Librarian, with the advice of the Executive Committee. The Outreach Librarian for Multicultural Services serves as an ex-officio member. In addition, the Committee is comprised of at least six members at-large. Members at-large are full- or part-time Library employees from both academic and support staffs, serve two-year staggered terms, and may be appointed to one successive term. The chair is appointed annually by the University Librarian. Additional members may be appointed to represent special concerns.

Membership

*Cindy Ingold, chair (08/15/11)
*Paula Carns (08/15/12)
*Kim Matherly (08/15/11)
Geoff Ross (08/15/12)
Gennye Varvel (08/15/11)
Pam Ward (08/15/12)

Emily Love (Outreach Librarian for Multicultural Services) *ex-officio*

Cindy Kelly, *ex-officio*

*second term

University Library
University of Illinois at Urbana-Champaign
1408 W. Gregory Dr. | Urbana, IL 61801
217-333-2290

For comments on this page contact: Gateway Conversion

Last modified by: Kimberley Matherly on 8/17/10

Diversity Committee

Current Membership

Library Human Resources Manager – Chair
Library Human Resources Program Assistant
Four library representatives appointed by the Dean of the Library

Purpose

The Committee exists to support the commitment of the University Library to equal opportunity and affirmative action by providing formal education, by assisting Library staff in the hiring process, and by serving as an informal resource.

Mission and Responsibilities

The Library Committee on Diversity works with the Dean of the Library to develop and promote a diverse work force within the ISU Library. The creation and maintenance of a community of women and men that is multicultural, multiracial, multinational and respectful of the dignity of all persons is essential to the educational mission of this library.

The Committee's role is:

1. To inform and educate Library personnel concerning diversity issues.
2. To maintain a focus on equal employment opportunity and affirmative action within the Library.
3. To help create a work environment in which all personnel are able to develop to the fullest extent of their potential.
4. To review with selection committees the recruitment process in relation to members of protected classes for professional positions, and to serve as a resource for hiring at all levels.

Organization

1. The Committee on Diversity will consist of not more than six members with the Human Resources Manager serving as Chair and the Human Resources Program Assistant serving as a standing member. The other four members will be appointed by the Dean to two-year terms, and may be reappointed once. Members will not ordinarily be reappointed for more than four consecutive years.
2. The Chair, with recommendations from the committee, will recruit new members by issuing a call for interested individuals then forwarding applications to the Dean. Vacancies should be filled as soon as possible.
3. The committee will be responsible to and report as needed through its Chair to the Dean of the Library.
4. Committee meetings will be called as needed by the Chair, a committee member, or the Dean of the Library. Brief minutes of each meeting will be routed to members. A permanent file of most recent committee papers will be in the custody of the chair, with older materials placed in the Archives collection.

Guidelines for the Committee on Diversity

Diversity Educators

1. Each year, the Committee on Diversity will identify possible staff development programs to educate Library personnel on all issues pertaining to diversity.
2. The committee, with the aid of the Human Resources office, will coordinate, publicize and host these programs.
3. The committee will educate library staff through articles in Inform, messages to all-users and/or material on the Intranet.
4. The committee will provide training and up-to-date guidelines for the selection process at all classification levels.

Faculty & P&S Search Processes

Faculty Search Committees

1. The Committee on Diversity will designate a representative to each faculty search committee to serve as a resource and advocate for equal opportunity and affirmative action issues; provide the search committee with pertinent background information; help the group to understand the library's commitment to equal opportunity and affirmative action.
2. The Committee representative will distribute EEO/AA information packets to search committee members at or before the first meeting of the search committee.
3. In an effort to assist the library in better affecting the principles of equal employment opportunity, the Committee representative is provided a fifteen-minute exit interview with each candidate.
4. The committee chair will keep a file documenting committee activities relevant to search
5. The committee representative will report to the Committee on Diversity chair and the Dean any concerns related to equal opportunity or affirmative action.

P&S Administrative Searches

The Committee on Diversity will provide the administrator responsible for each P&S search the EEO/AA information packet and serve as a resource for any questions related affirmative action and diversity.

Dean's Council
March 7, 2002 (revised 6/25/09)

Appendices

A. Diversity Outreach Collaborative Charge

Scope

The Diversity Outreach Collaborative will provide leadership and guidance throughout the UL by encouraging awareness about and discussions of diversity. Specifically, the Collaborative will focus on diversity issues with regard to UL climate, services to patrons, and campus outreach. This
Collaborative will act as an advisory group to the Diversity Outreach Librarian.

Context

In the wake of the University of Minnesota's transformation to become one of the top three research institutes in the world the need for support of diversity throughout the system has been identified as an important theme. During the strategic positioning process a System Wide Academic Task Force on Diversity was included. Beyond that, diversity was an issue that came up in almost every task force report concerning strategic positioning. It is felt that supporting diversity will contribute to faculty, staff and student retention through the creation of an inclusive supportive academic environment. It will also create a level of academic excellence that will assist in the University's goal to be one of the top three research institutions in the world.

The System Wide Academic Task Force on Diversity states, "Diversity should be defined as the full range of human difference that influences access, equity, and relationships in living, learning, and working environments. These differences have resulted historically in under-representation and marginalization based on race, ethnicity, gender identity/expression, sexual orientation, religion, disability, age, socioeconomic status, geography, and citizenship status. In other words, the University will be truly diverse when differences among individuals are leveraged to strengthen and enrich learning, working, and social environments, instead of being viewed as a negative condition."

The University of Minnesota has demonstrated its commitment to diversity by recently appointing Nancy "Rusty" Barceló as the first vice president and vice provost for equity and diversity. The Office for Multicultural and Academic Affairs has become the Office for Equity and Diversity (OED) and the units that report to this office are:

• Disability Services
• Equal Opportunity and Affirmative Action
• Gay, Lesbian, Bisexual and Transgender Programs Office
• Multicultural Center for Academic Excellence (it should be noted that the Diversity Outreach Librarian reports directly through this office.)
• Office for University Women

The University of Minnesota Libraries has demonstrated their commitment to diversity by creating the position of Outreach Librarian to Under Represented Groups in Academic Programs. The Outreach Librarian works in partnership with faculty and other campus professionals to develop programs that extend library collections and services to traditionally underserved populations, with an emphasis on multicultural programs and students of color, including international students.

8

Project Sponsor
Academic Programs
Karen Williams, AUL for Academic Programs
Jerilyn Veldof, Coordinated Education Services

Project Manager
Jody L. Gray, Diversity Outreach Librarian

Purpose / Focus

• Communicate regularly with Libraries staff. Establish a staff Wiki with diversity resources about various departments and roles on campus.
• Collaborate with the OED as well as the student services offices that report to OED (Multicultural Center for Academic Excellence, Disability Services, Gay, Lesbian, Bisexual and Transgender Programs Office, Office for University Women).
• Assess need for, develop and deliver campus programming in partnership with campus stakeholders.
• Develop a mechanism for ongoing environmental scan and inventory of issues, including attention to campus priorities, interests, and needs. Investigate what is happening in the colleges and create a basic inventory of these efforts. A wiki may be appropriate for this.
• Assist with the continued development of a campus climate and culture that supports and celebrates diversity.
• Serve in an advisory capacity to UL to meet diversity goals outlined in the University of Minnesota's Strategic Plan.
• Collaborate with and build coalitions among campus groups.
• Provide trainings for UL' staff to work with diverse populations.

Team members

Jody Kempf, PSE
Kimberly Clarke, SS&PP
Kate Brooks, A&H
Leslie Delserone, ABES
Claudia Sueyras, Libraries Residency Program
Rafael Tarrago, SS & PP

Consultants

Cody Hanson, CES
Jean Tretter, ASC
Su Chen, A & H

Project Stakeholders and Reviewers

• Academic Programs Directors
• Academic Programs staff
• Surrounding communities in Minnesota
• Libraries Organization Development Office
• University of Minnesota students, faculty and staff
• OED as well as the student services offices that report to OED (Multicultural Center for Academic Excellence, Disability Services, Gay, Lesbian, Bisexual and Transgender Programs Office, Office for University Women).

Initial Program Priorities 2008 and Timeframe
1. Advise Diversity Outreach Librarian on action plan for the UL to address the needs of the diverse student population at the University of Minnesota. This plan should align with the efforts that are being made throughout the rest of the University of Minnesota. (By first part of April 2008)
2. Identify key issues and collect data to determine which topics and initiatives should be addressed. Share knowledge and provide support and leadership to colleagues. Identify a small number of high impact or signature programs that the Libraries should initiate in the coming year. (By the end of April 2008)

Time Commitment
Will vary by project group. Collaborative members should plan to spend 2-4 hours per week on this work in the initial phase.

Budget
Budget requests developed as needed.

Collaborative Review
After the first year, the Sponsors will conduct a review of the Diversity Outreach Collaborative to determine if any changes need to be made to the group membership and/or its charter.
At this time it the sponsors will determine a rotation of members so that we always have some new and some continuing members on the group. Reviews will be conducted yearly thereafter.

9

UNIVERSITY OF MISSOURI

Diversity Action Committee

http://mulibraries.missouri.edu/staff/committees/affirmativeaction/default.htm

---

Site Index | Contact Us | Search: ___ [Go]

- Search Tools
- Course Resources
- About the Libraries
- Resources For...

Employee Directory
Forms Online
Library Policies

MU Libraries > Staff Web > Committees > Affirmative Action

Diversity Action Committee

"MU Libraries' services are based on the belief that sustained intellectual excellence is, in part, a direct result of diverse experiences and expressions interacting freely in an open society. Accordingly, the Libraries will follow recruitment, hiring, and promotion practices that guarantee equal opportunity for employment and advancement."

Introduction	Programs 2009-2010	Contact Us
Mission/Goals	Policy Documents	Related Links
Survey	Diversity Executive magazine	Annual reports and past programs

Updated MU Libraries' Diversity Mission/Goal Statements 8/08

MU LIBRARIES COMMITMENT TO DIVERSITY
As Missouri's leading public academic research library, the MU Libraries cultivates a welcoming environment for all members of the MU community, and will continue to support diversity, promote services, resources, and collections for an increasingly diverse society. We recognize diversity as a positive force that strengthens our abilities to solve problems, foster creativity, stimulate growth, pursue excellence, and continually increase the effectiveness of each of us.

MU LIBRARIES DEFINITION OF DIVERSITY
At the MU Libraries, diversity means accepting, respecting and valuing the differences of other human beings. MU Libraries celebrates the fact that each individual is unique, and acknowledges individual differences, including race, ethnicity, economic status, age, religious faith, sexual orientation, talent, abilities, geographic origin, political beliefs or cultural values.

MU LIBRARIES PROMOTES DIVERSITY IN THESE WAYS:
A) To support and promote the Libraries' diversity mission and to support the University's Diversity Initiative.
B) To act as a resource for employees, units, and divisions in achieving their diversity action goals.
C) To develop activities for diversity consciousness.

Copyright © 2007
MU Libraries, University of Missouri-Columbia
142 Ellis Library, Columbia, MO 65201-5149
Ph: (573) 882-4701

Contact the webmaster
EEO/ADA

Site Index | Contact Us | Search: ___ [Go]

- Search Tools
- Course Resources
- About the Libraries
- Resources For...

Affirmative Action Committee
Interview Packet
Introduction
Policy Documents
Bibliography
Related Links
Contact Us
Become a Librarian

MU Libraries > Library Staff > Committees > Affirmative Action > Introduction

Introduction

SCOPE OF DIVERSITY ACTION COMMITTEE

The Diversity Action Committee functions as an information resource and awareness group on behalf of the MU Libraries and its employees. Specific questions about the Committee may be directed to Leo Agnew HR Manager, or Jim Cogswell, Director of Libraries.

The Diversity Action Committee serves in an advisory capacity to the HR Manager. The Committee works with the HR Manager to develop diversity initiatives for the MU Libraries. The HR Manager serves as chair of the committee.

ANNUAL REPORTS TO MU HUMAN RESOURCES
2003   2004   2005   2006   2007
2008

Last updated: Jan. 22, 2009
Contact: Leo Agnew

Copyright © 2007
MU Libraries, University of Missouri-Columbia
142 Ellis Library, Columbia, MO 65201-5149
Ph: (573) 882-4701

Contact the webmaster
EEO/ADA

STAFF RESOURCES

Administration:
Cabinet, Committees, and Task Forces:

Libraries Advisory Committee on Diversity: Charge

The Libraries Advisory Committee on Diversity includes both library staff and faculty and is libraries-wide in scope. The Committee is charged with providing advice on issues of diversity. The overall goal of the library diversity program is to assure that all library personnel and library users feel welcomed, valued, and respected and to assure that library personnel, services, and collections appropriately reflect the diversity of the Rutgers community and its curriculum and research interests. To accomplish this, the Committee provides advice to the University Librarian on programs or policies affecting staff development, recruitment/retention, public services, and collections. The Committee works with the library faculty standing advisory committees, other library committees, and administrative offices as appropriate to carry out its charge.

Marianne I. Gaunt
University Librarian

Charge
Task Force On Diversity Recruitment Plan

The Task Force on Diversity Recruitment is charged with developing a five- year plan to increase the diversity of the faculty and staff of the University Libraries, and provide recommendations to insure that the Libraries attract a diverse pool of candidates for all positions. The plan should include:

- Methods for increasing the diversity of candidate pools (target programs/target groups), including successful practices elsewhere
- Changes needed in position profile descriptions, if necessary
- Placement of position postings if different from current practices
- Roles of and composition of search committees, especially in outreach, if different from current practices
- Recommendations for interview process changes, if necessary

The Task Force should consult existing documentation on library processes, diversity statistics of the university and nationally, the faculty handbook on diversity, and other materials and groups inside and external to the Libraries, as necessary.

Your report should be completed by April 30.

Members:

Lila Fredenburg, Director for Administrative Services, Chair
Judy Gardner, Interim Deputy Associate University Librarian for Research and Instructional Services
Triveni Kuchi, Chair of the Diversity Committee
Mark Winston, Assistant Chancellor and Director, Dana Library

02/09/10

Yale University Library

ABOUT THE LIBRARY

Departments & Staff / Working at the Library / Giving to the Library / Access & Use / Computers in the Library / Ask! a Librarian

Library Diversity Council

Purpose and Vision

The *Yale University Library Diversity Council* was formed in August 2005 to enhance the diversity and cultural competence of our staff so that our workplace continues to evolve into an even more inclusive and congenial environment. This type of atmosphere is conducive to job satisfaction and will in turn lead to even more effective service to our diverse patrons.

Diversity includes, but is not limited to, attributes such as age, gender, gender identity, sexual orientation, religion, race, national origin, cultural heritage, and ethnic background. Recognizing diversity is a key component of excellence in the workplace that allows individuals to reach their full potential.

The Diversity Council is taking a leading role in developing and implementing initiatives that promote diversity within our staff community.

Please take a look at our Strategic Plan 2009 - 2011 and Meeting Minutes, and feel free to call or email any of us with your comments and questions.

Meeting Minutes

- June 17, 2009
- June 2, 2009
- March 3, 2009
- January 6, 2009
- December 2, 2008
- November 4, 2008
- October 1, 2008
- June 4, 2008
- May 7, 2008
- April 2, 2008
- March 5, 2008
- February 6, 2008
- November 20, 2007
- October 17, 2007 - All Staff Meeting - Photograph of DC with Jerome Offord and Allison Sutton
- October 3, 2007
- September 12, 2007 - Welcome new members
- June 5, 2007
- May 16, 2007
- April 25, 2007 - Special Guest, Nydia Gonzalez, Yale University Chief Diversity Officer
- April 4, 2007

Members

Chair:

· **Mary Caldera**. Archivist, Manuscripts & Archives. Tel: 432-8019. mary.caldera@yale.edu

Immediate Past Co-Chairs:

· **Teresa Miguel**. Head of Foreign & International Law Reference, Law Library. Tel: 432-8023. teresa.miguel@yale.edu

· **Rich Richie**. Curator, South & Southeast Asia Collections. Tel: 432-1858. rich.richie@yale.edu

Council Members:

· **Frank Boateng**. Documents Asistant IV, Canadian Federal & FAO Collection, Government Documents. Tel: 432-3211. frank.boateng@yale.edu

· **Amy Burlingame**, Human Resources Supervisor and Staffing Representative, Library Administrative Services. Tel: 432-1810. amy.burlingame@yale.edu

· **Carolyn Hardin Engelhardt**. Ministry Resource Center Director, Divinity Library. Tel: 432-5319. carolynhardin.engelhardt@yale.edu

· **Gregory Eow**. Kaplanoff Librarian for American History and American Studies. Tel: 432-1757. gregory.eow@yale.edu

· **Dawn Ferguson** Library Acquisition Assistant III Sterling

Diversity Programs

Millenium Report Oversight Committee (MROC)

Documents, Resources & Past Events

UA Libraries Documents & Resources

On July 16, 2010, **Ricardo Andrade** (RSST) and **Danielle Walker** (AIST) presented a poster at the National Diversity in Libraries Conference at Princeton University. The poster was titled "Embedding Diversity Competencies in a Team-Based Workplace: An Innovative Approach of Continuous Learning at the U of Arizona Libraries."

Open House materials (June 2009):
1. MROC Response Team's Original Recommendations (from the June 2005 Report) {Grid for Follow-up}
2. MROC 2007/OCDA 2007/Focus Groups 2008 Results (April 2009) {Report}
3. MROC 2007/OCDA 2007/Focus Groups2008 Recommendations (June 2009) {Grid for Follow-up}
4. MROC *Draft* Additions to Guidelines for Selection Committees (June 2009) {Position Description, Diversity Competency, Interview and Reference Questions}

Millennium Report Oversight Committee (MROC) Response Team FINAL REPORT (June 2005) Janice Simmons-Welburn, Shelley Phipps, Dave Baca and Chestalene Pintozzi

Libraries Glossary of Diversity Terms

Nine Action Options

A More Accurate Way to Measure Diversity by Karen Stephenson and Valdis Krebs in *Personnel Journal*

Increasing Relevance, Relationships and Results: Principles & Practices for Effective Multicultural Communication--Library Edition written by Metropolitan Group

Past Events

April 28, 2009 (1:30-4:30 pm) or April 30 2009 (8:30-11:30 am) Main Library A313/4	*Racial Microaggressions.* An important workshop with J. Sarah Gonzales and Nhu Tien "Patty" Lu from the YWCA's Racial Justice Program-Tucson on the historical context of racism and the subtle yet commonplace slights and insults which demean a person's identity.

Handouts given out during the session:
- Racial Microaggressions Definition and Examples
- White Privilege Worksheet
- Speaking Up Against Bigotry

J. Sarah Gonzales, Director of Racial Justice Programs 884-7810 sgonzales@ywcatucson.org
http://www.ywcatucson.org
Related materials:

Racial Microaggressions in Everyday Life by Derald Wing Sue, et al
Racial Microaggressions and the Asian American Experience by Derald Wing Sue, et al
Racial Micraggressions against Black Counseling and Counseling Psychology Faculty by Madonna G.
Constantine, et al, in Innovations in Multicultural Research
Racism's Cognitive Toll: Subtle Discrimination is More Taxing on the Brain
Unmasking 'racial micro aggressions' by Tori DeAngelis in Monitor on Psychology
The Little Chill by Lise Funderburg in O the Oprah Magazine
Sweat the Small Stuff by Gloria Averbuch in NJMonthly
Why Your Boss May Treat You Right by Julie Rawe in Time Magazine
Book: *Micromessaging: Why Great Leadership is Beyond Word*s Stephen Young (McGraw-Hill 2006)

March 24 , 2008 (2-4 pm) Main Library A313/4	***Unconscious Bias Workshop.*** In follow-up to the UA's Banaji Workshop on Unconscious Bias in February, 2008, MROC held a session to talk about the concepts of unconscious bias and micro-meesaging as well as to foster and honor respect in the workplace, facilitated by Jeanne Kleespie, Asst. Vice President, UA Equal Opportunity and Affirmative Action Office, and Raji Rhys, Director, Diversity Resource Center.

Handouts and related resources:
Guidelines for Addressing Micromessaging
Hidden/Unconscious Bias: A Primer
Guidelines for Reducing the Impact of Unconscious Bias in the Workplace
Interview Toolkit
Unconscious Bias in Reading and Writing Evaluations
Unconscious Bias: Mentoring
Overview of Unconscious Bias Research
Exploring Unconscious Bias: The Millennial Student Project (impact on students)
The Implicit Prejudice article by Sally Lehrman from Scientific American May 22, 2006
Materials from the Banaji workshop: Powerpoint: Gender Bias in Science: Powerful but Invisible
mahzarin_banaji ...
Project Implicit: http://www.implicit.harvard.edu
Banaji website: http://www.people.fas.harvard.edu/~banaji/
Video Podcast of Banaji "Mind Bugs" Harvard University:http://www.people.fas.harvard.edu/~banaji
/research/mrb_talks/talks_by_year.htm
From Scientific American – Banaji Implicit Prejudice with Senior Executives
Resources collected by UA ADVANCE: http://www.advance.arizona.edu/resources.cfm#bias

January 23, 2008 AllSGA January 29, AllLFA, non-ranked appointed professionals	***Policies Sessions.*** Sessions facilitated by MROC's Chestalene Pintozzi and Laura Bender for SGA and LFA to explain questions about UA Libraries policies and guidelines identified in the 2007 Climate Survey.

Handouts given out during the session:
The Final (revised) MROC PowerPoint

December 1, 2006 1:00 p.m. - 3:30 p.m., Main Library A313/4	***A Dialogue About Civility: A Civil Conversation on Civility.*** an introduction to civility and respect with Joel Sadowski, Dances with Opportunity.

Handouts, notes and related background readings and web sites:
Notes from the Workshop - Ellen Lawrence-Barnes
Meditation on Civililty
Appreciative Inquiry Responses from group activity
Various handouts including Constructive Dialogue vs. Debate and Effective Listening
Brillante, Nicole and Peter Saunders. *Six Questions about Civility*. CIS Occasional
Paper 82.
Burgess, Guy and Heidi Burgess. *The Meaning of Civility*. Conflict Research
Consortium.
Public Conversations Project: PCP helps people with fundamental disagreements over divisive issues
develop the mutual understanding and trust essential for strong communities and positive action.

November 2, 2006 10 a.m. - 12 noon, Main Library A313/4	*Inclusive Excellence/Culture of Respect.* A compelling and thought provoking panel presentation from members of the UA student and faculty communities and the business community.

Handouts given out during the session:
By Amanda Simpson Transgender Definition Terms and Gender Identity
By Raji Rhys-Wietecha UA Discusses ... Creating Inclusive Learning Environments

June 8, 2006 (9 am- Noon for library leaders; 1:30-4:30 pm for Allstaff) Marriott University Park	*Redefining Diversity - What Does It Meant to Us?* An engaging dialogue on diversity and diversity managements concepts with Dr. R. Roosevelt Thomas, Jr., Founder and President of the American Institute for Managing Diversity and CEO of Roosevelt Thomas Consulting and Training.

Handouts given out during the session:
Powerpoint of the afternoon session: Empowering the Individual
Powerpoint of the morning session: Taking Diversity to the Next Level

Dr. R. Roosevelt Thomas Readings

Articles

From Affirmative Action to Affirming Diversity. *Harvard Business Review*, March/April 1990, Vol. 68 Issue 2, p107, 11p. (Full text available online through UA subscription – PDF attached)

Books

2006 *Building on the promise of diversity: how we can move to the next level in our workplaces, our communities, and our society.* New York: AMACOM/ American Management Association. HF 5549.5 M5 T463 2006

1999 *Building a house for diversity: how a fable about a giraffe & an elephant offers new strategies for today's workforce.* New York : AMACOM. HF 5549.5 M5 T462 1999 and NetLibrary

1996 *Redefining diversity.* New York: Amacom. HF 5549.5 M5 T464 1996 and NetLibrary

DISABILITY AWARENESS EVENT

OCTOBER 9, 2007
GELMAN LIBRARY
2130 H ST. NW
ROOM 207
11:30-2:30

THE GEORGE WASHINGTON UNIVERSITY
WASHINGTON DC

Special Thanks To:

Admin Group
&
GLS Diversity Group

Alicia Miller   John Danneker
Andrea Stewart   Kyle Compton
Antoinette Powell   Luke Drotar
Debra Guerra   Nia Phillips
Delia Rafuson   Noureen Kapadia
Emanuel Fang   Patricia Garcia
Katherine Gallemore   Sandra Carpenter
Emma Mosby   Shannon Holmes
Harry Prasetyo   Shirley Chang
Jing Zhong   Teena Bedola

★ ★ ★ ★ ★

NEXT DIVERSITY GROUP EVENT:

**HISPANIC HERITAGE CELEBRATION
TUESDAY, OCTOBER 16, 2007
GELMAN 207**

For more information, questions, or comments please contact:
Diversity@gelman.gwu.edu

PROGRAM

Welcome
Debra Guerra, Chair, Diversity Committee

Introduction of Melissa Bloomer and Andrea Cossettini
Emma Mosby

Lunch

Introduction of Jocelyn Hunter
Katie Gallemore

Closing Remarks
Debra Guerra, Chair, Diversity Committee

The Diversity Group was established to sponsor special events and exhibits that recognize and celebrate the global heritage and diverse cultural, social, and political perspectives that comprise the GW Community.

SPEAKERS

ANDREA COSSETTINI

Ms. Cossettini is currently completing a 4th year externship in audiology at the GW Speech and Hearing Center. She will earn a Doctor of Audiology degree from the University of Florida in May 2008.

She has a Masters degree from Northern Illinois University, in Anthropology. Her interest includes noise exposure; noise induced hearing loss, and hearing conservation.

Today, she will speak about the prevalence of hearing loss in the US, some of the things that prevent people from getting hearing help, and what difficulties someone with a hearing loss may encounter in daily interactions.

MELISSA BLOOMER FICHTER

Ms. Fichter is currently the Clinical Supervisor for Pediatric Autism and Social Language Clinic and Neurogenic Communication Disorders Clinic at GW Speech & Hearing Center and Adjunct Professor in the Speech and Hearing Science Department.

She earned her Master's Degree in Speech-Language Pathology, from GW. She has a Certificate of Clinical Competence (licensed) Speech-Language Pathologist.

Today she will provide us with a general overview of what the Speech & Hearing Clinic offers at GW. She will also provide a brief informational talk on the professional responsibilities/duties of a speech-language pathologist. She will briefly discuss the impact speech and language disorders have on individuals in all walks of life.

JOCELYN HUNTER

Ms. Hunter is Manager of Community Development at the Columbia Lighthouse for the Blind. Though diagnosed with Stargardt's Disease, a degenerative retinal disease at age 17, Ms. Hunter has excelled both professionally and personally. Prior to joining CLB, she worked in a variety of positions, including for Congressman Harold Ford. She also worked in the office of the NBA team, Memphis Grizzlies, and also as an officer on the University of Virginia's Honor Committee. Throughout life, Ms. Hunter has proven incorrect the many assumptions about the blind and visually impaired; she continues to educate and enlighten those around her about visual disability in a very unassuming way.

Today she will share her story as a young professional with a visual impairment and present information about the Columbia Lighthouse for the Blind.

Unit: ___U of L Libraries_____

Year: **2008-2009**

Diversity Activities Report List (Required Annually)

Activity	Date	Number of people attending	Diversity Category What unit diversity initiative was this activity addressing? (i.e., employees, students, climate, curriculum, training, & education)	How successful was this activity in addressing this initiative?	Will you continue to offer this activity?
Libraries sponsored the Kentucky Women's Book Festival with the Women's Center and the President's Office, providing space for the actual event and volunteers for the planning committee as well as the event itself.	February 2008	400	Education for faculty, staff, students, community	Successful	Yearly event, likely Libraries will participate again
Afghanistan Photography Exhibit (student exhibit)	January 2008	Exhibit open to all in library	Education for students, faculty, staff, and community	Successful	One time event
Forever Free exhibit	February 2008	Exhibit open to all in library	Education for students, faculty, staff, community	Successful	One time exhibit/event
Biofuels Exhibit for National Engineers Week	March 2008	Exhibit open to library visitors	Education for students, faculty, staff, community	Successful	Theme changes, but National Engineers Week exhibit is annual
Rare Books/Special Collections presentation at Liberty High School	March 2008	65	Student education/outreach	Successful	Yes
The Memory Keeper's Daughter Book Discussion w/Mary Karen Powers	March 2008	13	Education, faculty, staff, students		One time event
Launch of African American Oral History Collection (Digital Collections)	March 2008	Online collection-unlimited audience	Education for faculty, staff, students, community/general public	Successful	Yes

Set to Print Landscape on Legal Paper

15

Reflections: Jazz in Louisville- an exhibit, jazz performance, reception, and student art auction to benefit Instrumental Partners	April 2008		Education for students, staff, faculty; curriculum		One time event, but similar events possible
Banned Books Week	September 2008	Open to all in Library	Education, students, faculty, staff		Yearly event
Archivist provided consultation to Western Branch of the Louisville Free Public Library on preservation of their African American History Collection	September 2008	3	Community education and outreach	Successful	Yes, if asked to assist again
El Dia De Los Muertos- Day of the Dead exhibit	October 2008	Open to all in Ekstrom Library	Education for students, faculty, and staff	Successful	Yearly event
LGBT Pride Week exhibit of materials from the Williams Nichols Library and Archive for Lesbian, Gay, Bisexual and Transgender Studies	October 2008	Open to all in Ekstrom Library	Education, for students, faculty, staff	Successful	Similar exhibits possible
KLA/KSMA/SELA/ARL National Diversity in Libraries Conference- U of L Libraries were heavily involved with planning and also contributed by volunteering and presenting sessions on diversity & libraries during the conference.	October 2008	Approximately 900	Education for employees, community & profession	Successful	If offered again, Libraries will likely participate
Individual sessions are listed below.					
An Uncommon Learning Space			See above section on KLA/KSMA/SELA/ARL National Diversity in Libraries Conference		
Copyright in the Library Painless Solutions for the Moderately Squeamish			See above section on KLA/KSMA/SELA/ARL National Diversity in Libraries Conference		
Documenting Diversity in			See above section on		

Set to Print Landscape on Legal Paper

16

UNIVERSITY OF LOUISVILLE
2008–2009 Diversity Activities Report List
http://louisville.edu/library/diversity/plan.pdf

Activity	Date	Detail	Category	Result	Notes
Louisville			KLA/KSMA/SELA/ARL National Diversity in Libraries Conference		
Health Information Outreach at U of L			See above section on KLA/KSMA/SELA/ARL National Diversity in Libraries Conference		
International Students in Academic Libraries Designing User Services for the Global Campus			See above section on KLA/KSMA/SELA/ARL National Diversity in Libraries Conference		
Library 2.0, Social Networking, and You			See above section on KLA/KSMA/SELA/ARL National Diversity in Libraries Conference		
Librarians as Trail Guides: Pathways to the Workforce and Postsecondary Education			See above section on KLA/KSMA/SELA/ARL National Diversity in Libraries Conference		
The Black Experience in Library School			See above section on KLA/KSMA/SELA/ARL National Diversity in Libraries Conference		
The Ethical Implications of Library Instruction in a Multicultural Society			See above section on KLA/KSMA/SELA/ARL National Diversity in Libraries Conference		
The Impact of an Automated Storage and Retrieval System on Patron Services			See above section on KLA/KSMA/SELA/ARL National Diversity in Libraries Conference		
Director of OLT and Outreach librarian collaborated with the Crane House, the Asian Institute, Inc. to migrate the organization's library collection over to a web-based searchable catalog system.	2008		Community education/outreach	Successful	Additional projects are planned for 2009.
Archivist presented on sources at U of L for African American Genealogy Workshop, sponsored by Farmington Historic Plantation & Louisville Free Public Library	October 2008	50	Community education and outreach	Successful	One time event
African American Read-in & African American History exhibit.	February 2009	Open exhibit and read-in held in Ekstrom Lobby	Education for faculty, staff, students	Successful	Another event/exhibit is likely

Set to Print Landscape on Legal Paper

5. Develop professional development programs for staff that celebrate and promote equity and diversity

Actions	Assigned to	Stakeholders	Target Implementation Date
• Partner with Staff Education and Development and the OED • Develop a curriculum/outline/plan for cultural competency training for staff at the Libraries to support service to external communities	Staff Education and Development Diversity Outreach Librarian Diversity Outreach Collaborative	All units of the UL OED UL Communications	Spring 2009
Update			
Leslie Delserone attended a workshop put on by the EOAA Office on Intercultural Competencies. ***Developing Intercultural Skills and Competency (EO6010)*** *How do we communicate and work effectively in an environment where differences in "culture" lead to misunderstanding, conflict, and reduced productivity? Using the Intercultural Development Inventory (IDI), this introductory workshop is designed to help participants develop the skills to work and learn effectively in a multicultural environment. It also provides an overview of effective organizational responses to diversity in the workplace.* *Facilitators: Kimberly Simon; Lawrecina Mason Oramalu Audience: All interested University staff.* *Date: February 10, 2009 : 1:00 - 4:00 pm* *Location: 101 Walter Library* *Course Fee: $12.00* ABES is planning on arranging for this workshop to be delivered to their department in the upcoming months. They will report back how effective they have found this workshop.			

6. Provide diverse programming that promotes the understanding and celebration of differences as well as similarities

Actions	Assigned to	Stakeholders	Target Implementation Date
• Encourage celebrations, storytelling, and cross-cultural learning via staff events, speakers, as well as informal methods	All Units		Ongoing
Update			
Below is a list of some of the events that have taken place in the 2008-2009 academic year. This is not a comprehensive list. **Chicano/Latino Studies at the University of Minnesota** What: Exhibit: Chicano/Latino Studies at the University of Minnesota: Research Resources at Wilson Library When: February – March, 2009 Where: Wilson Library, basement level			

15

Archie Givens, Sr. (1919-1974) was a successful Minneapolis businessman and entrepreneur who was a strong supporter of higher education, particularly for young people of color. Come celebrate this man, his family, and the community that helped bring together a rich collection of African American literature and life.

Jean-Nikolaus Tretter and the Tretter Collection in Gay, Lesbian, Bisexual, and Transgender Studies
The Jean-Nickolaus Tretter Collection in Gay, Lesbian, Bisexual, and Transgender (GLBT) Studies is international in scope, devoted to the history and culture of the GLBT peoples, and covers all time periods.

Solar After Dark: Going Green At Night

What: The Spring 2009 Ada Comstock Distinguished Women Scholars Lecture
When: Tuesday, March 24, 2009 4:00 p.m.
Where: Cowles Auditorium, Hubert H. Humphrey Center
Free and open to the public.

Featuring Professor Jane H. Davidson
This award honors a University of Minnesota woman faculty member's exceptional research, scholarship, teaching, and leadership contributions via a public lecture.

Jane H. Davidson is passionate about renewable energy. A Professor of Mechanical Engineering, her current research focuses on solar systems for buildings, and solar thermo-chemical cycles to produce solar fuels. Professor Davidson has been recognized with the American Solar Energy Society Charles Greeley Abbot Award and the ASME John I. Yellott Award. Jane's presentation, "Solar after Dark: Going Green at Night," will focus on one of the most pressing challenges facing humankind--the need to drastically reduce greenhouse gas emissions while simultaneously meeting an exploding global demand for energy.

Dessert reception follows the lecture in the HHH Atrium.
Information about Ada Comstock and other awards at http://www.umn.edu/women

Presented by:
Women's Center, Office of Equity and Diversity
Office of the Senior Vice President for Academic Affairs and Provost
The Graduate School
University of Minnesota Libraries

International Education Week Library Information Fair a Success!
About 150 students attended the Library Information Fair last Tuesday and, as advertised, had many personal interactions with library staff from IADS and Academic Programs who introduced them to our library resources. We were joined by staff from the SMART Commons who also promoted their services. In addition, the Libraries' Diversity Outreach Collaborative used this opportunity to survey the international students about their specific library needs and will focus on addressing them.

Many thanks to all the staff from across the University Libraries who contributed to the Information Fair: Liya Ai, Mary Asp, Lynne Beck, Su Chen, Leslie Delserone, Julia Demasi (intern), Jan Fransen, Jody Gray, Martha Hardy, Charlie Heinz, Van Houlson, Tony Ihrig, Janice Jaguszewski, Jon Jeffryes, Lisa Johnston, Meghan Lafferty, Amy Lewis, Joung-Ah Park, Priscilla Pope, Scott Spicer, Maria Stracke, Phuoc Thi Minh Tran, Amy West, and Li Zhu.

Visit the IEW library web site at: http://sciweb.lib.umn.edu/infofair/ to view photos from the event.

7. Support and advocate for the inclusion of diversity-driven educational initiatives across campus

Actions	Assigned to	Stakeholders	Target Implementation Date
• Develop a way to formally submit diversity programming initiatives	Diversity Outreach Collaborative	All Units	Spring 2009

17

through the Diversity Outreach Collaborative • Develop a formal set of guidelines and program tools for library units to use in their work with diverse programs			
Update			
Below are several examples of the collaborations developed with UL and other University of Minnesota departments: LSAMP collaboration with Sci/Eng – beginning summer of 2007 and continuing – Contact Jody Kempf Summer Bridge to Academic Excellence – Libraries have partnered with this program since summer of 2007 – Contact Jody Gray Student Excellence in Academics and Multiculturalism (SEAM) – Libraries have partnered with this program since fall 2007 – Contact Jody Gray			

Strategy	Actions	Assigned to	Stakeholders	Target Implementation Date
Identify a small number of high impact or signature programs that the Libraries should initiate in the coming year.	•	Diversity Outreach Collaborative	AP, OED, Communications	Fall 2008
Update				
Peer Research Consultant pilot -Spring 2009 American Indian and African American Studies 40th Anniversary Exhibit – Fall 2009 Chicano/Latino Collections at the U Libraries Exhibit – Spring 2009 International Education Week Information Fair – Fall 2008 (Annual Event)				

18

2009-2010 Programs

There may be other events added to this calendar as those staff development opportunities become known. Additional information will appear in News Notes immediately preceding each program.

March 23, 2010 - A Discussion of the Civil Rights Act of 1964
Time: 3:00 – 4:30 p.m.
Place: Jesse Wrench Auditorium

The Civil Rights Act of 1964 celebrated its 45th year of enactment in 2009. Come hear three MU faculty members discuss the Act from three perspectives:

Dr. Charles Sampson, Truman School of Public Affairs, will talk about the political/social context in which the Act was passed.
Dr. Michael Middleton, Deputy Chancellor & Professor of Law, will provide an assessment of the impact of the Act for the first five years following its passage.
Dr. Jacquelyn Litt, Director of Women and Gender Studies, will share a current perspective and challenge the audience to think about other rights/protections that could be added to the Act.

Release time will be available with supervisor approval.

March 11, 2010 - International Tea and Snacks Break
Time: 3:00 - 4:00 p.m.
Place: Ellis Staff Lounge

Visit with colleagues as you sample teas and snacks from around the world. DAC will provide teas and some snacks; library staff will be asked to contribute snacks.

Tea flavors include:

Snacks include:

Release time is available with supervisor approval. RSVP's are not required.

November 5, 2009 - Developing Your Cultural Competency
Time: 1:00 - 4:00 p.m.
Place: 4F51-A Ellis Library
Trainer: Noor Azizan-Gardner, Manager of Diversity Programming, MU

The Census Bureau projects that by 2042, Americans who identify themselves as Hispanics, African Americans, Asians, Native Americans, Native Hawaiians and Pacific Islanders will together outnumber non-Hispanic whites (The New York Times, August 14, 2008).

Are universities and colleges around the country ready and able to engage with a truly multicultural population? It is time for us in libraries and educational institutions to take multiculturalism seriously and to jump to the next stage of becoming culturally competent. We are collaborators in developing students, who will, in turn, become culturally competent citizens of Missouri, the United States and the world.

What we know now through the last decade of research in the exciting field of intercultural communication is that a culturally competent environment requires the organization and all participants in it to engage in a process of mutual adaptation. Through a multimedia presentation and several experiential exercises, participants in the session will:

- explore the concept of culture and examine the culture of the university in general and the libraries in particular
- examine their cultural "self"
- learn about developing their cultural intelligence
- learn effective skills with colleagues and students through an understanding of differences in communication and conflict styles
- understand the current assimilation model and why we need to move to one of mutual adaptation
- explore next action steps to sustain this effort

October 27, 2009 - Library Issues Forum "Celebrating Intellectual Freedom: Reading, Writing, Speaking, and Creating"
Time: 8:30 - 10:00 a.m.
Place: S107 Memorial Union (Jesse Wrench Auditorium)
Panelists: Mary Barile, Ph.D. candidate, Theatre Department; and Mark Horvit, Executive Director, Investigative Reports and Editors at the School of

Journalism

The session wraps up the observance of Banned Books Week/Month and features several speakers with topics related to the theme of "Celebrating Intellectual Freedom: Reading, Writing, Speaking, and Creating." Release time is available with supervisor approval.

Mary Barile will provide an overview of the history of theatrical censorship. Mark Horvit will talk about issues faced by investigative reporters in terms of accessing and publishing information.

The Library Issues Forum was developed to fill a need for library employees to come together and talk about varied and broad library issues. If you have ideas for future forums, please contact Leo Agnew at AgnewL@missouri.edu.

September 30, 2009
Time: 1:00 - 2:00 p.m.
Place: Ellis Library, Collonade Area
Presenter: Charles Davis, Executive Director of f the National Freedom of Information Coalition at the School of Journalism

A part of Banned Books Week Celebrations, Charles Davis will talk about censorship and freedom of information.

August 4, 2009 - Library Issues Forum - Library Survey Results
Time: 8:30 - 10:00 a.m.
Place: S304 Missouri Unions
Presenter: Leo Agnew

Leo will share the results of the DAC diversity survey, the SDC survey on committee effectiveness, and the post-elephants training survey. Release time is available with supervisor approval.

July 21, 2009 - A visual representation of disability throughout history, research by Dr. Brick Johnstone, School of Health Professions/Health Psychology.
Time: 1:00 - 2:00 p.m.
Place: 4F51-A Ellis Library
Presenter: Dr. Brick Johnstone

Dr. Johnstone's research on the visual representation of disability throughout history offers an excellent opportunity to better understand the manner by which individuals with disabilities have been, and are currently, misperceived and mistreated in society. Review of art from prehistoric to modern times offers a wonderful opportunity to understand how misperceptions about physical, mental, and sensory disabilities have developed and been maintained throughout history.

Participants will have the opportunity to increase their understanding of the individual experience of disability. Given that 20% of the US population has a chronic disability, it is useful to provide a forum to mull over the possibility of our own potential misperceptions and biases. Release time is available with supervisor approval.

ALICE | InfoTree | FAQ | home

OHIO UNIVERSITY *Libraries*

ASK A LIBRARIAN ▶
im | chat | phone | e-mail | skype | appointment

Find   Services   Collections   Library Info

Culture Showcase Home Page
Current theme:
**International Student
Experience at Ohio U.**
  Speakers
  Bibliography

Previous themes:
  American Regionalisms
  Appalachian Women
  African American
   Heritage
  African American Studies
  & Alden Library
  Celebrating Firsts
  Presidential Politics
  Rites of Passage

Libraries' Diversity Program
Diversity Committee

The International Student Experience at Ohio University

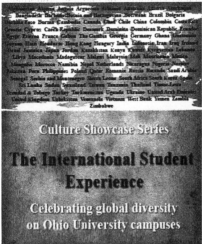

The number of international students attending Ohio University has increased significantly over the past several years. These students come from over 100 countries, with different languages, customs and cultures. The Libraries' spring Culture Showcase series will focus on the International Student Experience at Ohio University and the transition to a new environment for these students. We are planning two events for this spring, including a panel discussion of international students describing their experience coming to our university, as well as a guest lecturer.

The Libraries are working cooperatively with the Office of International Faculty and Student Services (ISFS) in developing the panel discussion. Three or four students, each from different countries, will talk about on their individual experiences coming to OHIO.

Also on the panel will be Krista McCallum Beatty, Director of ISFS, who will summarize the discussion and provide an overview of the international student experience.

Ohio University's Office of Institutional Research has produced tables of international student enrollment by country and major.

Speakers · Bibliography

Guide for International Students

Huan Ying   *Foon Ying*
Benvenuto   *Akwaba*
Willkommen   Merhaba
  Welcome   *Bienvenue*
Karibu   **Shagotawm**

Africana Librarian Araba Dawson-Andoh has written an online guide to International Student Resources. It provides basic information about the Libraries, database searching, and other useful information for students from other countries.

Archives & Special Collections | Fine Arts | Government Documents | International Collections | Music & Dance

OHIO University Libraries
Athens, OH 45701-2978
Phone: (740) 593-2699

Last updated: May 06, 2010
This page is maintained by the Diversity Committee.
Please use our Feedback Form for your questions, comments, and suggestions about the Libraries' services and resources.

PENNSTATE
UNIVERSITY | **LIBRARIES**

Diversity

2009/2010 Programs, Events and Exhibits

July 2009

7/30/09, "Civility@OurLibraries" Kickoff program to announce the initiative. Foster Auditorium and MediaSite.

August

September

9/28/09 - 10/25/09 - "Tradition is My Life: Education is My Future" - Artwork by American Indian and Alaska Native students (K-12), on display in the Diversity Studies Room, first floor, Pattee Library. This exhibit features the winning entries from an annual contest sponsored by the Office of Indian Education, U.S. Department of Education.

9/30/09, 3:00 - 4:00 PM, Foster Auditorium, 101 Pattee Library -Presentation "The American Indian Leadership Program at Penn State: Celebrating a 40-year Tradition of Leadership in Indian Education" by AILP Director and Professor of Education Dr. John Tippeconnic and Associate Professor of Education Dr. Susan Faircloth. This program is also on MediaSite Live: http://live.libraries.psu.edu/mediasite/Viewer/?peid=a5eba765f840432b80f2825b46ac91cf)

Penn State's American Indian Leadership Program (AILP) is the nation's oldest continuously operating educational leadership program for American Indians and Alaska Natives. Since 1970, more than 220 American Indian and Alaska Native students have earned master's and doctoral degrees from the program, and have gone on to pursue leadership positions at the local, tribal, state, and national levels. In this presentation, Dr. Tippeconnic and Dr. Faircloth will highlight AILP's achievements over the past four decades and talk about other anniversary-related events. They will also discuss some of the current opportunities and challenges facing American Indian schools and communities, and take questions from the audience.

October

10/5/09, 7:30 p.m.: "Hidden Voices: The Lives of LGBT muslims," HUB Auditorium. A presentation to dispel myths about Islam, explore diversity within the Muslim World, and shine light into the lives of an invisible and silent community. Presented by Faisal Alam. Co-sponsored by the LGBTA Student Resource Center and the University Libraries Diversity Committee.

10/22/09, 10-11:30 am, Foster Auditorium, "Hinduism: Principles, Beliefs, Traditions, and Practices." Come prepared with your questions! The University Libraries Diversity Committee has organized this special presentation in conjunction with the Hindu festival of Diwali (which falls on Oct. 17). Presenter Anil Kulkarni, a Penn State professor, will talk about Hinduism and answer your questions. Free and open to the public. Foster Auditorium, 101 Pattee Library. The presentation can also be viewed online at: http://live.libraries.psu.edu/mediasite/Viewer/? peid=22ff9d3755a245bb8ea6785f11a7e7c6 (Windows MediaPlayer required.)

10/26/09, 11am-12 noon, UL Diversity Strategic Plan Forum. Foster Auditorium and MediaSite.

November

11/17/09, 2:00-4:30 pm, Foster Auditorium, "The PITA Principle." This seminar focuses on the concept of "self-awareness" as a core ingredient to better interpersonal effectiveness with co-workers and customers. An honest self-assessment of strengths and growth areas can be a starting point for improvement. In their book, The PITA Principle: How to Work with and Avoid Becoming a Pain in the Ass (published in August of 2008), Drs. Orndorff and Clark high-light seven types of "PITAs" that are most prevalent in the workplace. This seminar offers practical strategies for working more effectively with each type of PITA and for becoming more aware of your own tendencies toward being difficult to work with in certain situations. *Sponsored by the University Libraries Civility Team

11/19/09, 3 - 4:30 pm, Foster Auditorium, 101 Pattee Library, "Global Perspectives" - Penn State study abroad and international students will share their experiences in a panel presentation and discussion titled "Global

Perspectives." This event is free and open to the public, and can also be viewed online: http://live.libraries.psu.edu/mediasite/Viewer/?peid=9090cf2d25ad47c58b7fd535492f68e9 The event is sponsored by the University Libraries Diversity Committee and Library Learning Services and is being held in conjunction with International Education Week (IEW). IEW is a joint initiative of the U.S. Department of State and the U.S. Department of Education. For more information, go to http://iew.state.gov/index.cfm. For more information on the presentation, contact Dawn Amsberry, dua4@psu.edu.

- Guide to University Libraries' Study Abroad and International Travel Resources.

December

12/2/09, 1-3:30 pm, Mann Assembly Room, "Assertive Communication: A Solutions-Based Approach." This workshop will focus on how to develop an assertive communication style. *Sponsored by the University Libraries Civility Team*

12/15/09, 1:00 - 3:00 pm, Mann Assembly Room, "Understanding the "T" in LGBT" - What does it mean to be transgender, transsexual? How can we as a university understand what individuals who identify as transgender experience and how can we support them? Presented by Allison Subasic, the current Director of the Lesbian, Gay, Bisexual, Transgender and Ally (LGBTA) Student Resource Center at The Pennsylvania State University and former Director of LGBTQ Services at the University of California, at Davis. Ms. Subasic is sought after nationally as a facilitator on LGBTQ issues. Originally from California, where she obtained a degree in sociology and social welfare from UC Davis, Ms. Subasic obtained a Masters Degree in Higher Education and College Student Affairs at Penn State. She has been presenting and teaching about differences and creating a welcoming environment for over fifteen years, specifically focusing on the issues and concerns facing the LGBTQ community. Ms. Subasic has presented at numerous conferences and workshops and believes in creating community through developing social justice allies. This event is co-sponsored by the University Libraries Diversity Committee and Libraries Human Resources.

January

Engaging Religious Diversity
Description

The religious landscape of the United States is changing, and this is having a dramatic effect on our workplaces, our schools and our communities. Those from other cultures and religious traditions bring a great wealth of knowledge to our country. Increased religious diversity, however, also means that there may be instances of clash. What systems and resources exist to engage the religious diversity that students, faculty and staff face in their professional lives and in the world? How do systems of privilege play out in the context of religious diversity? How do we manage an instance of religious clash in the workplace?

Objective

- Trends in religious diversity over the last five years

- Dominant stereotypes, myths and misunderstandings about religion and religious traditions
- Application of skill-based model to create sustained dialogue about religious differences and common ground
- Hot Spots for Conflict

Audience

- Library Staff

Approval Required	None
Delivery Type	Instructor Led
Fee	None

A class is not scheduled at this time. Please send us an email, and we will notify you as soon as a class has been scheduled.

Yale University Library
120 High Street
New Haven CT 06520 - 8240
203-432-1810(Phone)
203-432-1806(Fax)
andrew.gray@yale.edu
http://www.library.yale.edu/

This Website contains records of current and past training enrollments and requirements. Although the Training Requirements Assessment is intended to be as comprehensive as possible, training requirements may change, and there may be instances in which a training requirement applies to an individual who has not been flagged by questions in the assessment.

For missing or inaccurate data regarding training requirements, or if you think you may have answered an assessment question incorrectly, please contact the training requirement business unit directly. (Note: Business units are identified within each requirement description of the My Profile\My Requirements section of this Website.) For technical issues regarding the assessment or Website functionality, please email the TMS system administrator at: tmsadm@yale.edu.

Last modified: Thursday, December 3rd 2009

[Yulibl] Engaging Religious Diversity with Yale Divinity Alumnus, Vanessa Avery-Wall

Scrivani, Ernest ernest.scrivani at yale.edu
Tue Jul 15 10:32:45 EDT 2008

- Previous message: [Yulibl] REMINDER: Brown Bag 2.0 discussion TODAY 12:30pm
- Next message: [Yulibl] Information Commons ACRL webcast
- Messages sorted by: [date] [thread] [subject] [author]

Greetings.

There are still 8 seats available for the Engaging Religious Diversity, with Vanessa Avery-Wall of Hartford Seminary, tomorrow July 16th in the

Use this link register... https://medapps13.med.yale.edu/tms/tmscourses.get course details?p crs id=1404

Engaging Religious Diversity:
The religious landscape of the United States is changing, and this is having a dramatic effect on our workplaces, our schools and our communitie

Vanessa is a nationally recognized expert on issues of religious and international diversity. Engaged in the study of and religion and society i

Ernie

Ernie Scrivani
Yale University Library
Manager, Staff Training & Organizational Development
ernest.scrivani at yale.edu
203.432.1810

P please consider the environment before printing this email

-------------- next part --------------
An HTML attachment was scrubbed...
URL: http://mailman.yale.edu/pipermail/yulibl/attachments/20080715/cea486bb/attachment.html

---

- Previous message: [Yulibl] REMINDER: Brown Bag 2.0 discussion TODAY 12:30pm
- Next message: [Yulibl] Information Commons ACRL webcast
- Messages sorted by: [date] [thread] [subject] [author]

More information about the Yulibl mailing list

Come celebrate the beginning of a new year,
our diversity, and our achievements!!

WHEN: Friday, January 22, 2009
5:00 p.m. - 7:00pm
5:30 p.m. Presentation for Alice

WHERE: Sterling Memorial Library

WHAT TO BRING: You, your family, and a favorite dish
(no RSVP or tickets necessary)

WHO: The YUL International Party is
proudly sponsored by the
Library Staff Association (LiSA),
the YUL Diversity Council, and
Library Administrative Services (LAS)

Travel around the world and dine to the accompaniment of our resident staff musicians, enter our prize raffle, and join us in saying farewell to our University Librarian, Alice Prochaska. Guests are encouraged to dress in clothing representing our diveristy of backgrounds.

Recognizing the immense diversity of people and cultures that make up the YUL staff, we once again seek your culinary skills to provide tasty treats and dishes to represent your cultural heritage. Locations throughout Sterling will be used to offer these homemade dishes, each representing a different continent!

VOLUNTEERS NEEDED!
To volunteer your **Culinary Delights** please contact Ronel Namde (2-8379, ronel.namde@yale.edu)
To volunteer for **Set-up and/or Clean-Up** please contact Ian McDermott (2-2848, ian.mcdermott@yale.edu
Monetary Contributions can be brought to Jason Helms (2-8600, jason.helms@yale.edu)
Raffle Tickets can be purchased by any committee member or bought at the door.

Burlingame, Amy

From:	yulibl-bounces@mailman.yale.edu on behalf of Namde, Ronel [ronel.namde@yale.edu]
Sent:	Tuesday, January 19, 2010 10:46 AM
To:	yulibl@mailman.yale.edu
Subject:	[Yulibl] International Food- There is still time!!
Attachments:	ATT00001.txt

There is still time to decide to bring a dish!! We could still use some dishes from everywhere, so come and share your heritage and culture (or any favorite dish)!!

EINEN GUTEN RUTSCH INS NEUE JAHR

BONNE ANNÉE   HAPPY
NEW YEAR

حلول السنة الجديدة

The International Party is not quite a week away- what will you be bringing to share with your colleagues?!!

Happy New Year all!!
As in previous years, we will be setting up tables by continent- we would love to have a variety of food as representative as our staff!! Please consider sharing some of your heritage with us.

If you plan on bringing a dish, please keep in mind that RED LIQUIDS AND SAUCES and OPEN FLAMES are prohibited.

This year's International Party is January 22nd from 5:00-7:00 pm. So, decide on your dish soon and contact me with the ingredients list and what country you are representing.

If interested in providing a dish, please contact Ronel Namde at ronel.namde@yale.edu for more information.

Ciao!

-Ronel Namde

International Party Planning Committee

Ronel Namde
Conservation Assistant I
General Collections Conservation, Preservation Department
Yale University Libraries
130 Wall Street
New Haven, CT 06511
203.432.8739

 please consider the environment before printing this email

- March 7, 2007
- February 21, 2007
- February 7, 2007
- January 10, 2007
- December 13, 2006
- November 9, 2006
- October 25, 2006
- October 12, 2006

Other YUL Diversity Council Activities and Items of Interest

- **YUL International Party** - *February 27, 2009*, 5:00 - 8:00pm, SML - Please join us in celebration of the many diverse cultures, societies, and countries from where we originate.
- **Debbie Stanley-McAulay** - *February 27, 2009*, 11:00am - 12:30pm, SML Lecture Hall - Meet Yale's new Chief Diversity Officer and hear about the exciting goals and programs of the Office of Diversity and Inclusion. The presentation will be followed by a "meet and greet."
- **YUL Open House** - *June 7, 2008* - Presentation on Diversity Programs at YUL (pdf)
- **YUL International Party** - *February 29, 2008*, 5:30 - 8:00pm, SML - Please join us in celebration of the many diverse cultures, societies, and countries from where we originate.
- **Black History Month Lecture** with **Stephen Carter, J.D. '79** - *February 19, 2008*, 4:00pm, SML Lecture Hall. Prof. Carter is the author of several books, including *New England White*, *Reflections of an Affirmative Action Baby* and *The Emperor of Ocean Park*.
- **Queer Tea** - *February 12, 2008*, 4:00 - 6:00pm, SML Lecture Hall - help build community among the LGBTQ staff, faculty, students and their allies across Yale.
- **Dr. Brian Perkins**, SCSU Professor of Education and Chair of the Board of Education for the New Haven school system - *February 6, 2008*, 12 noon, SML Lecture Hall - Dr. Perkins will discuss the school system and various initiatives, including his role in increasing awareness of Africa through annual trips. Dr. Perkins will also reenact Dr. Martin Luther King's final speech.
- **New Haven!** *January 31, 2008*, 11:00 - 12 noon, SML Lecture Hall - Come learn the highlights of New Haven's culture, community and services. Hiring managers and others who participate in the recruitment process will come away armed with information and ready to answer that recruit's question, "So what does New Haven have to offer?"
- Co-sponsor **MLK Activities** - *January 18 - 21, 2008*
- **ALA Midwinter - Yale / ARL Initiative to Recruit a Diverse Workforce reception** - photographs from the conference (one, two)
- **Library School Fair** - co-sponsor with **SCOPA** - *October 18, 2007*, 1:30 - 3:30pm, SML Lecture Hall. Many library schools will be in attendance to share information about their programs, including distance-learning, financial aid, and scholarships. All are welcome!
- **All-YUL staff meeting** with **Jerome Offord, Jr., Director of Diversity Initiatives at ARL** - *October 17, 2007*, 3:00 - 4:30 pm, SML Lecture Hall. Reception to follow. All are welcome!

Acquisition Assistant in Sterling Memorial Library African Collection, Rm. 317. Tel: 432-1883
dawn.ferguson@yale.edu

· **Sarah S. Fisher**. Head, Printed Acquisitions Beinecke Rare Book and Manuscript Library Yale University. Tel: 432-2975.
sarah.fisher@yale.edu

· **Ahmed Ramadan**. Catalog Assistant, SML. Tel: 432-1800.
ahmed.ramadan@yale.edu

· **Patricia Thurston**. Cataloging, Assistant Head, Slavic Team. Tel: 432-8424.
patricia.thurston@yale.edu

· **Diane Turner**. AUL for Human Resources, Staff Training and Security. Tel: 432-1810.
diane.turner@yale.edu

· **Penny A. Welbourne**. Rare Book Team Catalog Department Yale University Library. Tel: 432-8378.
penny.welbourne@yale.edu

· **Matt Wilcox**, Epidemiology & Public Health Librarian, Director of Academic Technology Yale School of Public Health. Tel: 785-5680.
matthew.wilcox@yale.edu

- College Fair - *May 22, 2007*, SML Lecture Hall
- **GLBTQ Pride @ Yale** - *April 11, 2007*, SML Lecture Hall, 7pm - a Pride Week reading and discussion among three young queer authors with newly published works. More details here...
- **YUL International Party** - *February 23, 2007*, 5:00 - 8:00pm, SML
- Co-sponsor **MLK Activities** - *January 13 - 15, 2007*
- Co-sponsor, Lecture, **William Wright III** (photograph)
- Diversity Council Report to LMC (.ppt) - *November 16, 2006*
- Nota Bene, Spring 2006 (p.4)

Blogs

- Careers in Information, Librarianship, and Informatics (CHILI) Blog
  - CHILI poster - Will be unveiled at the Medical Library Association Annual meeting in Philadelphia on Tuesday, May 22, 2007
- Academic Library Diversity Blog at YUL

Yale Links

- **Electronic Bookshelf** - A selected bibliography of **Yale electronic resources on race and racism**
- Yale University appoints Chief Diversity Officer, Nydia A. Gonzalez, February 20, 2007
- Dean's Job Shifts to Focus on Diversity - Yale Daily News, February 2, 2007
- Yale University's Equal Opportunity Statement, as amended, October 17, 2006
- Provost's Initiative to Enhance Faculty Diversity
- Yale and Socioeconomic Diversity
- Yale College Multicultural Outreach Program
- Yale College - International Students
- LGBT Graduate Students
- LGBT Cooperative
- Psychology Department's Diversity Committee
- Diversity at the Yale School of Public Health
- Graduate School of Arts and Sciences - Office of Diversity & Equal Opportunity
- Yale Law School's Career Development Office Library - Diversity Resources

National Diversity Initiatives in Library Organizations and Library Schools

- ALA Office for Diversity
  - *Versed* - Official publication of the ALA's Office for Diversity; discussion of progressive practices in current library-based diversity work
  - Diversity Wiki - Collaborate, communicate, and connect with the most up-to-date information on diversity activities and issues that impact the profession
  - Diversity Events Wiki at the 2007 ALA Annual Meeting in Washington, DC
- ARL Diversity Initiative - Initiative to Recruit a Diverse Workforce - academic scholarships and career programs

Recruitment Programs

University of Delaware Library

Pauline A. Young Residency

The Pauline A. Young Residency offers recent recipients of a graduate library degree professional experience in a technology-rich, academic research library setting. The two-year residency is designed to meet both the professional goals and interests of the resident as well as the service and operational priorities of the University of Delaware Library. The 2010-2012 Residency features work in the Student Multimedia Design Center, a state-of-the-art multimedia facility with two instructional classrooms, four digital video studios, and more than 80 computers for individual and collaborative student use. The Center provides multi-level editing equipment and software, SMART boards to rehearse presentations, and more than 145 kits, such as video camera kits, for circulation.

The purpose of the residency is to increase the diversity of professional staff at the Library and to encourage the involvement of under-represented racial and ethnic minorities in academic librarianship. The residency forms one part of the Library's affirmative action plan and reflects the University of Delaware's strong commitment to affirmative action.

Opportunities

* explore current issues in academic librarianship
* flexible, individualized professional development plan
* structured and informal mentoring
* overview of the internal workings of an ARL library
* library committee service
* specialized training and workshops
* travel support for conferences of professional library organizations
* experience with latest information technologies

Qualifications

The University of Delaware Library seeks energetic, self-directed individuals interested in developing a career in academic librarianship. To qualify, applicants must have a recent graduate degree from an ALA-accredited program, previous public service experience, interest in multimedia technologies and instruction, strong written and oral communication skills, ability to work independently as well as the ability to work closely with colleagues and library users from diverse backgrounds. Members of under-represented racial and ethnic groups are encouraged to apply.

Salary and Benefits

The resident receives annual compensation at the level of Affiliate Assistant Librarian. Benefits include: vacation of 22 working days; liberal sick leave; generous flexible benefits program; TIAA-CREF or Fidelity retirement with 11% of salary contributed by the University; and tuition remission for dependents and course fee waiver for employee. University benefits brochure available at http://www.udel.edu/hr/Benefits_09_web.pdf. The Residency also provides both formal and informal mentoring opportunities along with travel support to attend conferences and professional meetings. Relocation assistance will be provided. This is a nonrenewable two-year appointment. The resident will be eligible to apply for available continuing positions in the University of Delaware Library.

| Residency Home Page | About the Program | The Environment | Application Information | Contact Information | Biographical Note | Program History | University of Delaware Library |

Academic Librarian Diversity Internship

About the Internship | Eligibility Requirements | Application Process

About the Internship

The **Academic Librarian Diversity Internship** is designed to introduce library students from historically underrepresented groups to careers in academic librarianship. The program underscores Kent State University's longstanding commitment to diversity and articulates the equally longstanding need within the profession of academic librarianship to recruit underrepresented librarian candidates. The program is designed to challenge library school students professionally and academically and offer a sound foundation for a career in academic librarianship.

The Academic Librarian Diversity Internship provides:

- 20 hour per week paid work assignment for 12 months within University Libraries (UL), providing an introduction to professional library work.

- The intern will receive a range of introductory experiences in the major operational units of a large academic research library. The intern may also have the opportunity to focus on and develop projects in a specific area of the academic library.

- A faculty mentor will be assigned to guide and advise the diversity intern.

- Additionally, the intern may have the opportunity to attend library

Diversity Internship

- About
- Requirements
- Application
- Program Flyer
- Office of Diversity

conferences.

Eligibility Requirements

Candidates must:

- Be a United States citizen and legally eligible to work.

- Demonstrate the character, motivation and ability to succeed based on their academic record, recommendations and personal statement on diversity.

- Demonstrate a commitment to academic librarianship and diversity based on their application and personal statement on diversity.

- Be an incoming or current student in an ALA-accredited LIS program.

Application Process

Application requires completion and submission of the following:

1. One-page application form ⬚.

2. A current resume or CV.

3. A one-page personal statement on diversity (see application form).

4. Official copies of transcripts for previous college coursework.

5. Two letters of recommendation that speak to the candidate's work history and/or academic achievements and committment to librarianship and diversity.

Deadlines: Applications for the 2010-2011 Diversity Internship must be postmarked by 2 April 2010. Finalists will be contacted for interviews in April 2010.

Questions: For questions, please contact Mary Lovin at 330-672-4483 or by email.

| Home | Research | Services | About Us | Help | Contact Us | Search | Site Index | Personal |

Icon Legend/Key: ⬚ Off-Site Link   ⬚ PDF File   * Required Form Field

This page may be found at: http://www.library.kent.edu/diversity_internship

Page last updated: 2010-07-09

Privacy Statement

©2003-2010 University Libraries

Mobile Site

Email this page...

Questions or comments about this page?

Contact Library - Assistance/Information

The University of Louisville Libraries' Diversity Residency Program seeks a recent MLS graduate who is interested in a career in academic librarianship. (To learn about the Libraries' commitment to diversity, see http://library.louisville.edu/diversity/.) This program is designed to provide the Resident with individually designed opportunities for learning and working in several different library settings, while contributing to the overall success of the University Libraries. The Resident will work in a challenging environment in several functional areas, supervised by a home department for each rotation while being guided by an assigned Mentor.

Responsibilities: May include assignments in Technical Services, Reference, Special Collections, Archives, the Oral History Center, the Copyright Office, and/or with digital projects. Current proposals for various rotations throughout the libraries are available at http://library.louisville.edu/diversity/residency. In consultation with the Mentor, the Resident will be placed in two to four units based on professional interests, skills, and relevant work experience. The Resident will serve as a member of the Diversity Task Force and after the first six months may participate in other committee work if interested. The Resident will be evaluated yearly by the same process as tenured and tenure-track faculty. The Resident can apply for travel funds and is encouraged to attend conferences, give presentations and write for professional publications.

Required Qualifications:
- Recent graduate (with less than three years professional experience) from an ALA-accredited Master's degree program,
- Interest in a career in academic librarianship
- Demonstrated commitment to diversity
- Good critical thinking skills
- Ability to commit to goals and achieve established outcomes
- Strong interpersonal, oral, and written communication skills
- Ability to work collaboratively in a team environment as well as the ability to work independently
- Knowledge of reference services, sources, and principles of instruction
- Familiarity with basic technical services
- Basic familiarity with copyright issues
- Knowledge of information and digital technologies
- Commitment to professional achievement and growth

Environment: The University of Louisville Libraries (http://library.louisville.edu) became a member of the Association of Research Libraries (http://www.arl.org) in 2002, reflecting their stature as a major research library system. The University of Louisville (http://louisville.edu) is a Carnegie I research university with a national reputation for high-quality undergraduate programs, more than twenty nationally recognized research, graduate, and professional programs, and a strong commitment to the community in which it resides. It is Kentucky's metropolitan university, serving over 21,000 students in the largest urban area in the commonwealth with a mission "to foster and sustain an environment of inclusiveness" (http://louisville.edu/provost/diversity/). The city of Louisville (http://louisvilleky.gov/) offers hospitality, warmth, and smaller city advantages like less traffic, shorter commutes and lower cost of living with major city amenities like world-class performing arts, great sports, incredible dining and a nationally-acclaimed parks system.

Salary and Benefits: Minimum $37,000 annually, with appointment rank, and salary commensurate with experience. UofL offers a comprehensive benefits package, including 22 days annual leave, tuition remission for six credit hours per semester, several options for health and retirement plans and a selection of other options. This is a non-tenure track faculty position on a yearly contract, renewable for up to three years.

Application Procedure: Submit an online application via UofL Human Resources web site at http://louisville.edu/jobs/ (Job ID #21723.) In addition send a cover letter addressing the listed qualifications and your interest in the position, unofficial graduate transcripts and the names, addresses, phone numbers and email addresses of three references to:

Katherine Burger Johnson, Associate Professor
400 Ekstrom Library, University of Louisville, Louisville, KY 40292
phone: (502) 852-6674   fax: (502) 852-6673   kbjohnson@louisville.edu

Applications received by December 1, 2007 will be given first consideration in the initial screening, but applications will be accepted until the position is filled. Position is available immediately, but the starting date is negotiable.

The University of Louisville is an Equal Opportunity/Affirmative Action Employer
committed to cultural diversity.
Women and minorities are encouraged to apply.

 NCSU **LIBRARIES**

NCSU Libraries *Focus Online*

Volume 23 number 3 - Spring 2003

Peer Research Advisors Make the Difference

By Megan Oakleaf and Amy VanScoy, Research and Information Services, and Karen Letarte, Cataloging

Patrons of the NCSU Libraries will notice some fresh new faces at the reference desk this semester. Douglas Brooks, Carlos Villate, and Patrice Williams are three NC State undergraduate students who are participating in the new Peer Research Advisors program, which was developed by the Libraries' Diversity Committee and modeled on successful programs at other institutions. Peer research advisors are students from diverse backgrounds who are interested in helping fellow students while improving their own research skills. They help answer questions at the reference desk and assist librarians with instruction sessions and outreach efforts. The Peer Research Advisors program aims to:

- present a welcoming and diverse face of library public services to students;
- develop the peer research advisors' information literacy skills and contribute to their academic success;
- enhance the ability of all undergraduates to use the library effectively; and
- recruit young, diverse people into librarianship.

Many interested students applied for the program, and the three students chosen are ideal candidates. All three are enthusiastic, service oriented, and interested in the library. Douglas Brooks, from Pittsboro, North Carolina, is a junior majoring in electrical engineering. Brooks applied to the program to "assist those people who find it difficult to do research in such a large facility." He has enjoyed "every minute" of the program and is "impressed with the enthusiasm and effort that goes into library research."

Carlos Villate, a senior majoring in biological sciences, has lived in Puerto Rico; Ludwigsburg, Germany; and Fayetteville, North Carolina. Villate plans to be a military intelligence officer in the United States Army after graduation. He likes the library's work atmosphere and the learning opportunities the Peer Research Advisors program provides, and the amount and complexity of library resources impress him. Villate says, "In my short time here I have learned so much."

Patrice Williams of Goldsboro, North Carolina, is a junior majoring in business management who plans to attend graduate school. Williams was attracted to the Peer Research Advisors program because it involves technology and research. She felt that it fit her personality because she loves to put puzzles together, and she finds the work educational and fun. Williams adds, "I thought I knew it all, but I learn every time I step into work."

The students joined the Peer Research Advisors program this spring semester and have received library training in a variety of subject areas including chemistry, engineering, and specialized techniques for government documents. The students have also learned about some of the Libraries exciting services and initiatives by attending presentations on the Digital Media Lab, the Assistive Technologies Center, LOBO (the Libraries' online research tutorial), and electronic reserves. These advisors are beginning to use their new skills and knowledge to answer user questions on their own. As they discuss the interactions they have had at the reference desk and in the classroom, it is clear they are beginning to understand the challenges and thrills of assisting users in a research library. As one peer research advisor said, "Many students I know have said they have never been to the library before, and I just think they are missing a lot."

The Peer Research Advisors program is one of a number of library initiatives to make students aware of the excellent career possibilities in library and information science. There is a critical need for librarians worldwide, and there are excellent graduate programs in this field in the Triangle area. The Libraries hopes the program will develop into an important part of its services, provide intellectually challenging jobs for students, and encourage some of NC State's exceptional undergraduates to join the profession.

Job Descriptions

Outreach Librarian for Multicultural Services
University of Illinois Library at Urbana-Champaign

Position Available: August 16, 2006. A full-time tenure track, or tenured position with the rank of Assistant or Associate Professor of Library Administration.

Duties and Responsibilities: The University of Illinois at Urbana Champaign is seeking an experienced public service librarian to provide focused support for the delivery of library services and resources to diverse populations across campus. The Outreach Librarian for Multicultural Services will report directly to the Associate Librarian for Services and is responsible for the development, implementation, and assessment of multicultural programs and initiatives for the University Library. This librarian will work formally with those university offices and specific academic programs that support education across all cultural and ethnic groups on campus. The incumbent will also work with a variety of student groups on campus to keep them informed of Library programs and to collaborate on ways to bring more services to those groups. Within the library system, the Outreach Librarian for Multicultural Services will work collaboratively with various subject selectors to develop programs and services. With an office in the undergraduate library, the librarian will also work closely with the Undergraduate Library Instruction Coordinator and with the Coordinator for Information Literacy Services and Instruction to develop the capacity for the Library to support the diverse learning initiatives on campus. The incumbent will be a member of the User Education Committee and is formally part of the Central Public Services Division of the Library.

Environment: The University of Illinois at Urbana-Champaign is committed to excellence, and its emphasis on diversity is a vital part of that commitment. In a university, the enrichment of knowledge through exposure to many cultures is vital to the missions of teaching, research, and service. The University of Illinois at Urbana-Champaign is dedicated to creating an environment that celebrates diversity and fostering a campus climate that has a place for each person, a place from which each person can explore the rich tapestry of knowledge.

The University of Illinois Library at Urbana-Champaign is one of the preeminent research collections in the nation and the world. With more than 10 million volumes and a total of 21 million items, it ranks third among academic libraries in the United States and first among public university libraries in the world. As the intellectual heart of the campus, the Library is committed to maintaining the strongest collections and services possible and engaging in research and development activities—both of which support the University's mission of teaching, research, and public service. The Library currently employs approximately 100 faculty and 300 staff members. For more detailed information, please visit http://www.library.uiuc.edu/.

The Library consists of more than 40 departmental libraries that are located throughout campus and administratively organized into eight divisions. One of the largest UIUC libraries, the Undergraduate ("Undergrad") Library, serves as a logical point of introduction to the larger University Library system; the website address is http://www.library.uiuc.edu/ugl. The Undergrad Library collection has been developed to support undergraduate coursework and research and to encourage the full use of the scholarly resources available throughout the University Library. The Undergraduate Library collection includes over 250,000 books, 320 current magazine and journal subscriptions, 3,200 reserve items, and over 75,000 non-print items.

Librarians collaborate with campus faculty and staff to develop instruction that is responsive to teaching and learning needs and furthers the development of student information literacy. The programs are characterized by assessment of student learning outcomes and systematic program evaluation and particular attention is paid to identifying unserved and underserved groups.

Qualifications: Required: Accredited Masters Degree in Library Science, with direct experience in providing service to a diverse academic community. Experience with program development and management of library outreach programs as well as knowledge of current and emerging technologies. Evidence of ability to perform research, achieve publication, and engagement in university/professional/community service in order to meet the University's standards for promotion and tenure. Ability to work in a heterogeneous and multi-unit environment. Demonstrated oral and written communication skills. **Preferred:** Knowledge of one or more of the following subject areas: Afro-American Studies, Asian American Studies, Latino/Latina Studies, Native American Studies or other multicultural research areas. Ability to speak Spanish or reading knowledge of another language of the major U. S. immigrant groups is preferred. Library instruction experience, and experience with computer-aided instruction (CAI), and other multimedia applications **Desired:** Demonstrated experience in grant project design, writing and implementation.

Salary and Rank: Salary is competitive and is commensurate with experience and credentials. This is a full time faculty appointment at the rank of Assistant or Associate Professor, depending on service and research record.

Terms of Appointment: Twelve-month appointment; 24 work days vacation per year; 11 paid holidays; 12 annual sick leave days (cumulative), plus additional 13 days (non cumulative) per year if necessary; health insurance, requiring a small co-payment, is provided to employees (coverage for dependents may be purchased); participation in the State University Retirement System which includes several private options including TIAA-CREF, is compulsory upon appointment (8% of the staff member's salary is withheld on a pre-tax basis, and is refundable upon termination); newly hired university employees are covered by the Medicare portion of Social Security, and are subject to its deduction.

Campus and Community: The University of Illinois at Urbana-Champaign is a comprehensive and major public land-grant university (Doctoral/Research University-Extensive) that is ranked among the best in the world. Chartered in 1867, it provides undergraduate and graduate education in more than 150 fields of study, conducts theoretical and applied research, and provides public service to the state and the nation. It employs 2,000 faculty members who serve 26,000 undergraduates and 10,000 graduate and professional students; approximately 25% of faculty receives campus wide recognition each year for excellence in teaching. More information about the campus is available at http://www.uiuc.edu.

The University is located in the twin cities of Champaign and Urbana, which have a combined population of 100,000 and are, situated about 140 miles south of Chicago, 120 miles west of Indianapolis, and 170 northeast of St. Louis. The University and its surrounding communities offer a cultural and recreational environment ideally suited to the work of a major research institution. More information about the community can be found at http://www.cucvb.org, http://www.ccchamber.org/.

Apply: Send letter of application and complete resume with the names, addresses, and telephone numbers of three references to: Cindy Kelly, Head, Library Human Resources, University of Illinois Library at Urbana-Champaign, 1408 W. Gregory Drive, Suite 127, Urbana, Illinois, 61801, (217) 333-8168. E-mail mokelly@uiuc.edu. Electronic applications are acceptable initially, but must be followed by a hard copy with signature.

Deadline: March 1, 2006. To ensure full consideration applications must be received by the deadline date.

**THE UNIVERSITY OF ILLINOIS IS AN AFFIRMATIVE ACTION/
EQUAL OPPORTUNITY EMPLOYER**

North Carolina State University Libraries

ACADEMIC PERSONNEL LIBRARIAN
Vacancy Announcement

Between the mountains of the Blue Ridge and the shores of the Outer Banks lies North Carolina's Research Triangle of Raleigh, Durham, and Chapel Hill. One of the nation's premier concentrations of academic, corporate, and public research, the area combines moderate year-round temperatures, rolling hills, championship college athletics, and a rich diversity of cultural events. The Triangle consistently ranks high on lists of desirable American communities, including a recent rating as the number-one place to be in terms of education and standard of living. The North Carolina State University Libraries has been recognized as the first recipient of the Association of College and Research Libraries' *Excellence in Academic Libraries Award* for its teamwork, innovation, and continuous interaction with students and faculty to further the educational mission of NC State University. The NCSU Libraries is ranked 29th by the Association of Research Libraries among North America's top 113 academic research libraries.

The NCSU Libraries invites applications and nominations for the position of **Academic Personnel Librarian** to provide leadership for the Libraries' recruiting program and for its diversity initiatives. In a library that is actively engaged in defining the future of librarianship, the Academic Personnel Librarian plays a key role in the recruitment, development, and retention of library employees and in educating others about careers in academic research libraries.

Responsibilities
Develops and implements innovative initiatives to recruit and retain highly qualified individuals to positions in the NCSU Libraries and to the profession of librarianship. Directs the nomination, search, and appointment processes for all professional positions. As an ex-officio member on nomination committees, serves as policy and procedures expert, insuring compliance with federal regulations and university policies, including Equal Opportunity and Affirmative Action. Collaborates with librarians, managers, and administrators to develop and enhance retention efforts. Establishes and maintains liaison relationship with graduate faculty in top MLS programs throughout North America, visiting schools, placement centers, and selected conferences.

Plans and implements programs that foster a climate where diverse staff and user populations feel welcomed, valued, and respected. Develops and implements strategies to increase employment and retention of members of underrepresented groups. Represents the Libraries in campus, regional, and national diversity efforts. Participates in planning, serves on library-wide committees, task forces, and teams. Librarians at NCSU Libraries are expected to be active professionally and to contribute to developments in the field. Reports to the Associate Director for Organizational Design and Learning.

Qualifications **Required**: ALA-accredited MLS or equivalent advanced degree in library or information science. Two or more years' professional experience in an academic library. Demonstrated knowledge of relevant employment laws and regulations. Excellent interpersonal and presentation skills; demonstrated excellence in oral and written communications. Ability to exercise judgment and handle personnel matters with discretion. Experience using current technology, including database and Internet applications. Evidence of organizational skills and ability to work effectively on an independent basis and as a member of a team. Evidence of ability for ongoing professional development and contribution. Willingness and ability to travel. **Preferred**: Experience with diversity programming. Formal training or education in relevant employment laws, regulations, and practices.

SELECTED RESOURCES

Books and Journal Articles

Acree, Eric Kofi, Sharon K. Epps, Yolanda Gilmore, and Charmaine Henriques. "Using Professional Development as a Retention Tool for Underrepresented Academic Librarians." *Journal of Library Administration* 33, no. 1 (2001): 45–61.

American Library Association. *Bridging Boundaries to Create a New Workforce: A Survey of Spectrum Scholarship Recipients, 1998–2003.* 2006.

Anaya, Toni, Charlene Maxey-Harris, and Anchalee Panigabutra-Roberts. "Strategies for Diversity Initiatives: A Case Study at University of Nebraska-Lincoln Libraries." In *Recruitment, Development, and Retention of Information Professionals: Trends in Human Resources and Knowledge Management*, edited by Elisabeth Pankl, Danielle Theiss-White and Mary Bushing, 46–61. Hershey, PA: Business Science Reference, 2010.

Aronson, David. "Managing the Diversity Revolution: Best Practices for 21st Century Business." *Civil Rights Journal* 6 (Winter 2002): 46–71.

"Best Practices in Diversity Planning and Assessment." *ASHE Higher Education Report* 33, no. 1 (2007): 89-102.

Black, William K., and Joan M. Leysen. "Fostering Success: The Socialization of Entry-Level Librarians in ARL Libraries." *Journal of Library Administration* 36, no. 4 (2002):3–27.

Bonnette, Ashley. "Mentoring Minority Librarians Up the Career Ladder." *Library Administration & Management* 18, no. 3 (2004): 134–39.

Cultural Diversity Programming in ARL Libraries. SPEC Kit 165. Washington, DC: Association of Research Libraries, 1990.

Dewey, Barbara I., and Jillian Keally. "Recruiting for Diversity: Strategies for Twenty-First Century Research Librarianship." *Library Hi Tech* 26, no. 4 (2008): 622–29.

Dewey, Barbara I., and Loretta Parham. *Achieving Diversity: A How-to-do-it Manual for Librarians.* New York: Neal-Schuman Publishers, 2006.

Evans, Alvin, and Edna Breinig Chun. "Are the Walls Really Down? Behavioral and Organizational Barriers to Faculty and Staff Diversity." *ASHE Higher Education Report* 33, no. 1 (2007): 1–139.

Gray, Jody. "A Different Approach to Diversity Outreach." *College & Research Libraries News* 71, no. 2 (2010): 76–79.

Groves, Christy, and William Black. "Making the Best of the Best: Strategies for Effective Retention." In *Recruitment, Development, and Retention of Information Professionals: Trends in Human Resources and Knowledge Management,* edited by Elisabeth Pankl, Danielle Theiss-White, and Mary Bushing, 218–31. Hershey, PA: Business Science Reference, 2010.

Hall, Tracie D. "Best Practices for Placing Diversity at the Center of Your Library." In *Achieving Diversity: A How-to-do-it Manual for Librarians,* edited by Barbara I. Dewey and Loretta Parham, 33–45. New York: Neal-Schuman Publishers, 2006.

Howland, Joan. "Beyond Recruitment: Retention and Promotion Strategies to Ensure Diversity and Success." *Library Administration & Management* 13, no. 1 (1999): 4–13.

Kreitz, Patricia A. "Best Practices for Managing Organizational Diversity." *Journal of Academic Librarianship* 34, no. 2 (2008): 101–20.

Lowry, Charles B., and Paul J. Hanges. "What is the Healthy Organization? Organizational Climate and Diversity Assessment: A Research Partnership." *portal: Libraries and the Academy* 8, no. 1 (2008): 1–5.

Mestre, Lori. *Librarians Serving Diverse Populations: Challenges and Opportunities.* Chicago: Association of College and Research Libraries, 2010.

Minority Recruitment and Retention in ARL Libraries. SPEC Kit 167. Washington, DC: Association of Research Libraries, 1990.

Neely, Teresa Y., and Lorna Peterson. *Achieving Racial and Ethnic Diversity Among Academic and Research Librarians: The Recruitment, Retention, and Advancement of Librarians of Color.* A White Paper by the ACRL Board of Directors Diversity Task Force. October 2006.

Neely, Teresa Y., and Megan K. Beard. "Recruiting and Retaining Academic Research Librarians: Post-MLS Residency Programs." *College & Research Libraries News* 69, no. 6 (2008): 314–15.

Neely, Teresa Y. "Assessing Diversity Initiatives: The ARL Leadership and Career Development Program." *Journal of Library Administration* 49, no. 8 (2009): 811–35.

Smith, Paula. "Culturally Conscious Organizations: A Conceptual Framework." *portal: Libraries & the Academy* 8, no. 2 (2008): 141–55.

Young, Courtney L. "Collection Development and Diversity on CIC Academic Library Web Sites." *Journal of Academic Librarianship* 32, no. 4 (July 2006): 370–76.

University Diversity Plans

University of Arizona
Diversity Action Plan
http://diversity.arizona.edu/pdf/diversity%20action%20plan.pdf

University of California
University of California Diversity Statement
http://www.universityofcalifornia.edu/diversity/diversity.htm

UCLA Strategic Plan for Diversity
http://www.diversity.ucla.edu/strategicplan/index.htm

University of Delaware
The Path to Prominence through Diversity
http://www.udel.edu/aboutus/diversity-finalreport.pdf

University of Louisville
University-wide Diversity Planning
http://louisville.edu/diversity/university-wide-diversity-planning.html

North Carolina State University
University Diversity Plans and Initiatives
http://www.ncsu.edu/diversity/planning/

Oklahoma State University
Institutional Diversity
http://diversity.okstate.edu/

University of Rochester
Diversity at the University
http://www.rochester.edu/diversity/

Virginia Tech
Principles of Community
http://www.vt.edu/diversity/

Human Resources Documents

University of Arizona
Employment at the UA Libraries and the Center for Creative Photography
http://www.library.arizona.edu/about/employment/index.html

University of British Columbia
Employment Equity Policy No. 2 (University of British Columbia)
http://www.universitycounsel.ubc.ca/policies/policy2.pdf

Advertising of Position Vacancies Policy No. 20 (University of British Columbia)
http://www.universitycounsel.ubc.ca/policies/policy20.pdf

UBC Statement on Respectful Environment for Students, Faculty and Staff
http://www.hr.ubc.ca/files/pdf/UBC_RES_PDF_2008.pdf

University of Manitoba
Overview of Equity Procedures of Academic Recruitment
http://www.umanitoba.ca/admin/audit_services/media/Overview_EP.pdf

703 Manual. Procedures and Guidelines for Academic Recruitment
http://www.umanitoba.ca/admin/human_resources/equity/703_manual/703_manual.html

York University
Employment Equity
http://www.yorku.ca/hr/units/employmentequity/index.html

Employment Equity Policy
http://www.yorku.ca/univsec/policies/document.php?document=14

Accommodation in Employment for Persons with Disabilities
http://www.yorku.ca/secretariat/policies/document.php?document=2

Workplace Climate Assessment

Pennsylvania State University
2008 Faculty/Staff Survey. Diversity Results
http://facultystaffsurvey.psu.edu/documents/FacultyStaffSurvey-NewswireArticle2.pdf

University of Rochester
Annual Report on Diversity
http://www.rochester.edu/diversity/annualreports.htm

Virginia Tech
Virginia Tech Climate Survey, 2009
http://www.hr.vt.edu/files/file_hr_Climate_Survey_Fall_2009.pdf

Yale University
Workplace Survey
http://www.yale.edu/hronline/conversations/

6224902R0

Made in the USA
Charleston, SC
28 September 2010